Best Garden Plants *for* Ontario

(handwritten: from your "son" and daughter-in-law!)

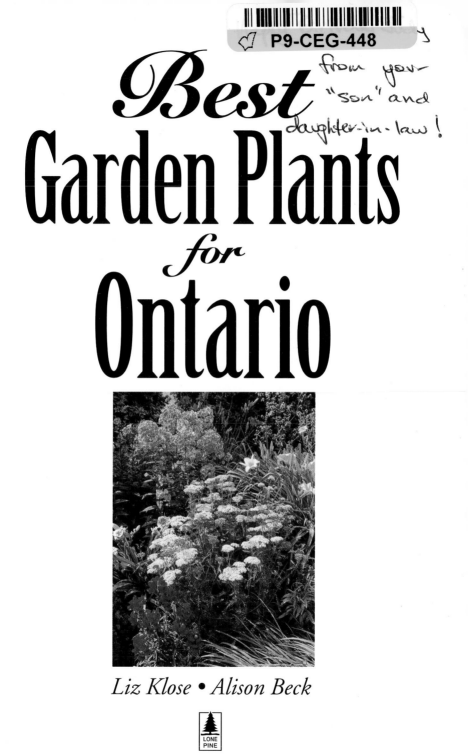

Liz Klose • Alison Beck

Lone Pine Publishing

The Publisher: Lone Pine Publishing

10145 – 81 Avenue
Edmonton, AB T6E 1W9 Canada
Website: www.lonepinepublishing.com

1808 B Street NW, Suite 140
Auburn, WA, USA 98001

Library and Archives Canada Cataloguing in Publication

Beck, Alison, 1971-
    Best garden plants for Ontario / Alison Beck, Liz Klose.

Includes index.
ISBN-13: 978-1-55105-477-3.   ISBN-10: 1-55105-477-9

    1. Plants, Ornamental--Ontario. 2. Gardening--Ontario.
I. Klose, Liz, 1959- II. Title.

SB453.3.C2B438 2005   635.9'09713   C2004-905747-2

Editorial Director: Nancy Foulds
Project Editors: Gary Whyte, Rachelle Delaney
Photo Coordinator: Don Williamson
Illustrations Coordinator: Carol Woo
Production Manager: Gene Longson
Book Design & Layout: Heather Markham
Image Editing: Trina Koscielnuk, Elliot Engley
Cover Design: Gerry Dotto
Scanning & Electronic Film: Elite Lithographers Co.

Photography: All photos by Tamara Eder and Tim Matheson except AAFC 84b; Bailey Nursery Roses 128a; Janet Davis 81b; Don Doucette 138b, 145a&b; EuroAmerican 13, 37a; Jen Fafard 148a; Erika Flatt 9b, 98a, 114b, 143a, 144b, 149a, 166b; Lynne Harrison 139a; Horticolor 134b; J.C. Bakker & Sons Ltd. 84a; Duncan Kelbaugh 144a; Liz Klose 31b, 48a&b, 64a, 127a, 151a, 152a, 153a&b, 158a, 161a, 162a, 165a, 170a&b, 172a; Dawn Loewen 70a, 82a; Janet Loughrey 81a; Marilynn McAra 148b, 150a; Kim O'Leary 31a, 74a, 100a, 146a, 155b; Allison Penko 10b, 22a, 39a, 40a, 57a, 65b, 78a, 97b, 106a&b, 109b, 112b, 114a, 133b, 139b, 142b, 143b, 147a, 163a&b, 164a, 165b, 169; Laura Peters 9a, 10a, 43a&b, 47a, 65a, 95b, 149b, 151b, 152b, 154a&b, 157a&b, 158b, 161b, 162b, 164b, 166a, 168a&b, 172b; Robert Ritchie 49a, 52a&b, 101a, 104a, 118a, 129a, 138a, 155a; Leila Sidi 150b; Joy Spurr 134a; Peter Thompstone 19a, 27a, 54a, 63a&b, 67a; Mark Turner 74b; Don Williamson 138b, 145a&b.

This book is not intended as a "how-to" guide for eating garden plants. No plant or plant extract should be consumed unless you are certain of its identity and toxicity and of your potential for allergic reactions.

We acknowledge the financial support of the Government of Canada through the Book Publishing Industry Development Program (BPIDP) for our publishing activities.

PC: P1

Table of Contents

A big bouquet of thanks to the following for their inspiration and passion for plants: the staff and students at the Niagara Parks Botanical Gardens and School of Horticulture and in particular, Darrell Bley, Instructor/Curator of Woody Plants, who enthusiastically co-authored the Trees and Shrubs section; Martin Quinn and Catherine Macleod; and to our families and friends, we are forever grateful for your encouragement.

This book is intended to cultivate your growing desire to learn more about the best plants for Ontario and empower you to put the "right plant in the right place."

Introduction

Starting a garden can seem like a daunting task, but it is also an exciting and rewarding adventure. With so many plants to choose from, the challenge is deciding which ones and how many to include in your garden. This book is intended to give novice gardeners the information they need to start planning and planting gardens of their own. It describes a wide variety of plants, provides basic planting and growing information and offers plant use tips to help you produce a beautiful and functional landscape.

Ontario has a temperate climate; the summer growing season is long and warm and the winters are cold enough to ensure a good period of dormancy and plenty of flowers in spring. Rainfall is fairly predictable and the soil, though not without its challenges, supports a variety of healthy plants.

Hardiness zones and frost dates are terms often used when discussing climate and gardening. Hardiness zones consider factors that influence the growing conditions, including winter weather, precipitation, humidity and summer temperatures. Plants are rated based on the zones in which they grow successfully. Though Canada's zones are similar to the hardiness zones developed in the United States, they are not identical. The last frost date in spring and the first frost date in fall allow us to predict the length of the growing season and when we can begin planting out in spring.

Microclimates are small areas that are generally warmer or colder than the surrounding area. Buildings, fences, trees and other large structures can provide extra shelter in winter, but may trap heat in summer, thus creating a warmer microclimate. The bottoms of hills are usually colder than the tops, but may not be as windy. Take advantage of these areas when you plan your garden and choose your plants; you may even grow out-of-zone plants successfully in a warm, sheltered location.

Getting Started

When planning your garden, start with a quick analysis of the garden as it is now. Plants have different requirements and it is best to put the right plant in the right place rather than to change your garden to suit the plants you want.

Knowing which parts of your garden receive the most and least amounts of sunlight will help you choose the proper plants and decide where to plant them. Light is classified into four basic groups: full sun (direct, unobstructed light all or most of the day); partial shade (direct sun for about half the day and shade for the rest); light shade (shade all or most of the day with some sun filtering through to ground level); and full shade (no direct sunlight). Most plants prefer a certain amount of light, but many can adapt to a range of light levels.

The soil is the foundation of a good garden. Plants use the soil to hold themselves upright, but also rely on the many resources it holds: air, water, nutrients, organic matter and a host of microbes. The particle size of the soil influences the amount of air, water and nutrients it can hold. Sand, with the largest particles, has lots of air space and allows water and nutrients to drain quickly. Clay, with the smallest particles, is high in nutrients but has very little air space. Water is therefore slow to penetrate clay and slow to drain from it.

Soil acidity or alkalinity (measured on the pH scale) influences the amount and type of nutrients available to plants. A pH of 7 is neutral; a lower pH is more acidic. Most plants prefer a soil with a pH of 5.5–7.5. Soil-testing kits are available at most garden centres, and soil samples can be sent to testing facilities for a thorough analysis. These tests will give indicate which plants will do well in your soil and what kind of soil amendments you should make.

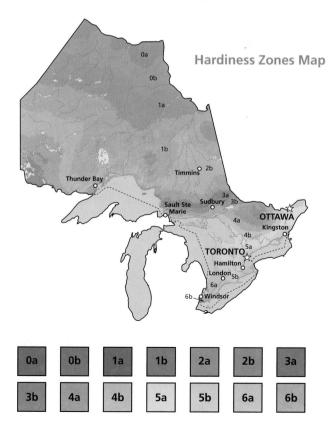

Hardiness Zones Map

0a	0b	1a	1b	2a	2b	3a

3b	4a	4b	5a	5b	6a	6b

Compost is one of the best and most important amendments you can add to any type of soil. Compost improves soil by adding organic matter and nutrients, introducing soil microbes, increasing water retention and improving drainage. Compost can be purchased or you can make it in your own backyard.

Selecting Plants

It's important to purchase healthy plants with no pests or diseases. Such plants will establish quickly in your garden and won't introduce problems that may spread to other plants. You should have a good idea of what the plant is supposed to look like—the colour and shape of the leaves and the habit of the plant—and then inspect the plant for signs of disease or insect damage.

Most plants are container grown. This is an efficient way for nurseries and greenhouses to grow plants, but when plants grow in restricted spaces for too long, they can become pot bound, with their roots densely encircling the inside of the pot. Avoid purchasing plants in this condition; they are often stressed and can take longer to establish. It is often possible to remove pots temporarily to inspect the roots. You can check for soil-borne insects and rotten roots at the same time. Pot-bound roots must be lightly pruned or teased apart before planting.

Planting Basics

The following tips apply to all plants.
• Prepare the garden before planting.
Remove weeds, dig or till the soil if you are starting a new landscape and make any needed amendments. This may be more difficult in established beds to which you want to add a single plant. The prepared area should be the size of the plant's mature root system.
• Unwrap the roots. It is always best to remove any container before planting to give roots the chance to spread out naturally when planted. In particular, you should remove plastic containers, fibre pots, wire and burlap before planting trees. Fibre pots decompose very slowly, if at all, and wick moisture away from the plant. Burlap may be synthetic, which won't decompose, and wire can eventually strangle the roots as they mature. The only exceptions to this rule are the peat pots and pellets used to start annuals and vegetables; these decompose and can be planted with the young transplants. However, you should still slice the sides of a peat pot and remove any part of it that will be exposed aboveground to prevent the pot from wicking water away from the roots.
• Accommodate the rootball. Your planting hole, prepared ahead of time, will only need to be big enough to accommodate the rootball with the roots spread out slightly.
• Know the mature size. Plant based on how big the plants will grow rather than their size when you plant them.

1. Gently remove container.

2. Ensure proper planting depth.

3. Backfill with soil.

Large plants should have enough room to mature without interfering with walls, roof overhangs, power lines, walkways and other plants.

- Plant at the same depth. Most plants generally like to grow at a certain level in relation to the soil and should be planted at the same level they were at in the pot or container before you transplanted them.
- Settle the soil with water. Good contact between the roots and the soil is important, but if you press the soil down too firmly, as often happens when you step on the soil, you can cause compaction, which reduces the movement of water through the soil and leaves very few air spaces. Instead, pour water in as you fill the hole with soil. The water will settle the soil evenly without allowing it to compact.
- Identify your plants. Keep track of what's what in your garden by putting a tag next to each plant when you plant it. A gardening journal is also a great place to list the plants you have and where you planted them. It is very easy for novice and seasoned gardeners alike to forget exactly what they planted and where they planted it.
- Water deeply. It's better to water deeply once every week or two, depending on the plant, rather than to water a little bit more often. Deep and thorough watering forces roots to grow as they search for water and

helps them survive dry spells when water bans may restrict your watering regime. Containers are the exception to the watering rule; they can dry out quickly and may even need watering every day. Always check the rootzone before you water because some soils hold more water for longer periods than other soils. More gardeners over-water than underwater. Mulching helps retain moisture and reduces watering needs.

Choosing plants

When choosing plants, aim for a variety of sizes, shapes, textures, features and bloom times. Features like decorative fruit, variegated or colourful leaves and interesting bark provide interest when plants aren't blooming. This way, you will have a garden that captures your attention all year.

Annuals

Annuals are planted new each year and are only expected to last for a single growing season. Their flowers and decorative foliage provide bright splashes of colour and can fill spaces around immature trees, shrubs and perennials.

Annuals are easy to plant and are usually sold in small cell-packs of four or six. The roots quickly fill the space in these small packs, so the small rootball should be broken up before planting. I often split the ball in two up the centre or run my thumb up each side to break up the roots.

4. Settle backfilled soil with water.

5. Water the plant well.

6. Add a layer of mulch.

Many annuals are grown from seed and can be started directly in the garden once the soil begins to warm up.

Perennials

Perennials grow for three or more years. They usually die back to the ground each fall and send up new shoots in spring, although they can also be evergreen or semi-shrubby. They often have a shorter period of bloom than annuals, but require less care.

Many perennials benefit from being divided every few years, usually in early spring while plants are still dormant or, in some cases, after flowering. This keeps them growing and blooming vigorously, and in some cases controls their spread. Dividing involves digging the plant up, removing debris, breaking the plant into several pieces using a sharp knife, spade or saw and replanting some or all of the pieces. Extra pieces can be shared with family, friends and neighbours. Consult a perennial book such as *Perennials for Ontario* for further information on the care of perennials.

Trees & Shrubs

Trees and shrubs provide the bones of the garden. They are often the slowest-growing

Roses are lovely on their own or in mixed borders.

plants, but usually live the longest. Characterized by leaf type, they may be deciduous or evergreen, and needled or broad-leaved.

Trees should have as little disturbed soil as possible at the bottom of the planting hole. Loose soil settles over time and sinking even an inch can kill some trees. The prepared area for trees and shrubs needs to be at least two to four times bigger than the rootball.

Staking, sometimes recommended for newly planted trees, is only necessary for trees over 1.5 m (5') tall. Stakes support the rootball until it grows enough to support the tree itself. Stakes, tied to the trunk 60–90 cm above the ground, allow the trunk to move with the wind.

Pruning is more often required for shrubs than trees. It helps them maintain an attractive shape and can improve blooming. Consult a book, such as *Tree and Shrub Gardening for Ontario*, for pruning information.

Roses

Roses are beautiful bushes and shrubs with often-fragrant blooms. Traditionally, most roses only bloomed once in

Trees and shrubs provide backbone to the mixed border.

Training vines to climb arbours adds structure to the garden.

Lilies bloom throughout the summer.

the growing season, but many new varieties bloom all summer. Repeat blooming, or recurrent, roses should be deadheaded to encourage flower production. One-time bloomers should be left alone; colourful hips will develop.

Generally, roses prefer fertile, well-prepared planting areas. A rule of thumb is to prepare an area 60 cm (24") across, front to back and side to side, and 60 cm (24") deep. Add plenty of compost or other fertile organic matter and keep roses well watered during the growing season. Many roses are durable and adapt to poor conditions. Grafted roses should be planted with the graft at least two inches below the soil line. When watering, avoid wetting the foliage to reduce the spread of blackspot.

Roses have specific pruning requirements. Consult a book like *Roses for Ontario* for detailed information.

Vines

Vines or climbing plants are useful for screening and shade, especially in a location too small for a tree. They may be woody or herbaceous and annual or perennial. Some vines physically cling to surfaces, while others have wrapping tendrils or stems. Still others may need to be tied in place with string.

Sturdy trellises, arbours, porch railings, fences, walls, poles and trees are all possible vine supports. If a support is needed, ensure it's in place before you plant to avoid disturbing the roots later. Choose a low-maintenance support that suits the vine you are growing. It should be sturdy enough to hold up the plant and it should match the vine's growing habit—clinging, wrapping or tied.

Bulbs

These plants have fleshy, underground storage organs that allow them to survive extended periods of dormancy. They are often grown for the bright splashes of colour their flowers provide. They may be spring, summer or fall flowering. Each has an ideal depth and time of year at which it should be planted.

Hardy bulbs can be left in the ground and will flower every year. Some popular tender plants are grown from bulbs, corms or tubers and are generally lifted from the garden in late summer or fall as the foliage dies back. Store these bulbs in a cool, frost-free location for winter, and replant them in spring.

Many herbs grow well in pots.

Herbs

Herbs have medicinal, culinary or other economic purposes. A few common culinary herbs are included in this book. Even if you don't cook with them, their fragrance will fill your garden and the plants can be quite decorative in form, leaf and flower. A container of your favourite herbs placed in a convenient location—perhaps near the kitchen door—will yield flavour and fragrance all summer.

Ornamental grasses add colour, variety and texture.

Many herbs have pollen-producing flowers that attract butterflies, bees, hummingbirds and predatory insects to your garden. Predatory insects feast on problem insects such as aphids, mealy bugs and whiteflies.

Foliage Plants

Many plants are grown for decorative foliage rather than flowers. Some of these are included in other sections of this book, but we have recognized a few with foliage that adds a unique touch to the garden. Ornamental grasses, ferns, groundcovers and other foliage plants bring a variety of colours, textures and forms to the landscape.

Ornamental grasses and grass-like plants provide interest all year, even in winter when the withered blades are left to stand. Cut them back in early spring and divide them when the clumps begin to die out in the centre.

A common sight in moist and shady gardens, ferns provide a lacy foliage accent and combine well with broad-leaved perennials and shrubs. Some ferns will survive in full sun.

Groundcovers, although the term can be used to describe any plant, are low-growing plants used to fill in spaces. They suppress weeds, blend plantings together, mask bare ground and provide alternatives to turfgrass where it won't grow or where it's difficult to maintain.

A Final Comment

The more you discover about the fascinating world of plants, whether it be from books, talking to other gardeners and appreciating their creative designs, or experimenting with something new in your own garden, the more rewarding your gardening experience will be. This book is intended as the seed from which your passion for plants can grow.

Ageratum
Ageratum

*A*geratum is an amazing butterfly magnet. It offers a constant supply of nectar to many butterfly species throughout summer and fall.

Growing
Ageratum flowers best in **full sun** but tolerates partial shade. The soil should be **fertile, moist** and **well drained**. This plant doesn't like to have its soil dry out; a moisture-retaining mulch will reduce the need for water.

Tips
The smaller varieties, which are often completely covered with fluffy flowerheads, make excellent edging plants for flowerbeds and pathways. They are also attractive grouped in masses or grown in planters. The taller varieties work well in the centre of a flowerbed or interplanted with other annuals. They also make interesting cut flowers.

Recommended
A. houstonianum has clusters of fuzzy blue, white or pink flowers and forms a large, leggy mound that can grow up to 24" tall. Many cultivars are available; most, including the **Danube** and **Hawaii Series**, have a low, compact form that makes a popular choice for border plantings. Others, including the **Horizon Series** and **'Leilani'**, are much taller and make good cut flowers.

A. houstonianum (above & below)

Ageratum blossoms are extraordinarily long-lived.

Also called: floss flower **Features:** flowers, habit **Flower colour:** white, pink, mauve, blue, purple **Height:** 15–90 cm (6–36")
Spread: 15–45 cm (6–18")

Angelonia
Angelonia

A. angustifolia 'Alba' (above), A. a. 'Blue Pacific' (below)

Angelonia is in the same botanical family as snapdragon (Antirrhinum), another popular summer annual known for its vibrant flower colours.

With its loose, airy spikes of orchid-like flowers, angelonia makes a welcome addition to the garden.

Growing

Angelonia prefers **full sun** but tolerates a bit of shade. The soil should be **fertile, moist** and **well drained**. Although this plant grows naturally in damp areas such as along ditches and near ponds, it is fairly drought and heat tolerant. Plant out after the chance of frost has passed. Pinch plants back at planting time to encourage bushier growth. Deadhead the entire flower spike once all the flowers are spent.

Tips

Angelonia makes a good addition to an annual or mixed border and looks most attractive when planted in groups. It is also suited to a pondside or streamside planting.

Recommended

A. angustifolia is a bushy, upright plant with loose spikes of flowers in varied shades of purple. The flowers resemble snapdragons, but are more delicate. Cultivars with white or bicoloured flowers are available.

Also called: summer snapdragon, angel wings **Features:** attractive flowers **Flower colour:** purple, blue, white, bicoloured **Height:** 30–60 cm (12–24") **Spread:** 30 cm (12")

Bacopa
Sutera

Bacopa snuggles under and around the stems of taller plants, forming a dense carpet dotted with tiny, white to pale lavender flowers. It cascades over pot edges to form a waterfall of stars.

Growing

Bacopa grows well in **full sun to partial shade**, although protection from the hot afternoon sun is advised. The soil should be of **average fertility, humus rich, moist** and **well drained**.

Don't allow this plant to dry out or its leaves will quickly die. Cutting back dead growth may encourage new shoots to form.

Tips

Bacopa is a popular choice for hanging baskets, mixed containers and window boxes. It can be used as a sprawling bedding plant, but it performs best in containers. Keep plants consistently moist during hot weather.

Recommended

S. cordata is a compact, trailing plant that bears small white flowers all summer. Cultivars with larger white flowers (**'Giant Snowflake'**), lavender flowers (**'Lavender Showers'**) or gold and green variegated foliage (**'Olympic Gold'**) are available.

Bacopa will thrive as a houseplant in a bright room.

S. cordata 'Giant Snowflake' (right)

Features: decorative flowers, foliage and habit **Flower colour:** white, lavender **Height:** 8–15 cm (3–6") **Spread:** 30–50 cm (12–20")

Begonia
Begonia

B. Rex Cultorum Hybrids 'Escargot' (above)
B. x tuberhybrida (below)

With its beautiful flowers, compact habit and decorative foliage, there is sure to be a begonia to fulfill your gardening needs.

Growing
Light shade or **partial shade** is best, though wax begonias and some tuberous begonias perform well in full sun if their soil is kept moist. The soil should be **fertile, rich in organic matter** and **well drained** with a **neutral** or **acidic pH**. Allow the soil to dry out slightly between waterings, particularly for tuberous begonias. Begonias love warm weather, so don't plant them before the soil warms in spring. If they sit in cold soil, they may become stunted and fail to thrive.

Tips
All begonias are useful for shaded garden beds and planters. The trailing tuberous varieties can be planted in hanging baskets and along rock walls where the flowers will cascade over the edges. Wax begonias have a neat, rounded habit that makes them particularly attractive edging plants. Rex begonias, with their dramatic and decorative foliage, are useful as specimen plants in containers and beds.

Recommended
B. Rex Cultorum **hybrids** (rex begonias) are grown for their dramatic, colourful foliage.

B. x *sempervirens-cultorum* (wax begonias, fibrous begonias) have pink, white, red or bicoloured flowers and green, bronze, reddish or white-variegated foliage. Bronze-leaved selections are more sun tolerant.

B. x *tuberhybrida* (tuberous begonias) are generally sold as tubers and are popular because they have flowers in many shades of red, pink, yellow, orange and white.

Features: colourful flowers, decorative foliage
Flower colour: pink, white, red, yellow, orange, bicoloured or picotee **Height:** 15–60 cm (6–24") **Spread:** 15–60 cm (6–24")

Black-Eyed Susan
Rudbeckia

R. hirta 'Becky Mixed' (above), *R. hirta* (below)

lack-eyed Susan brightens up any spot in the garden, and its tolerance for heavy soils makes it useful in new developments where the topsoil is often very thin.

Growing
Black-eyed Susan grows equally well in **full sun** and **light shade**. The soil should be of **average fertility, humus rich, moist** and **well drained**. This plant tolerates heavy clay soil, sandy soil and hot, dry weather. If it is growing in loose, moist soil, black-eyed Susan may reseed itself. Deadhead to prolong blooming.

Tips
Plant black-eyed Susan individually or in groups, in beds and borders, large containers, meadow plantings and wild-

flower gardens. This plant will bloom well, even in the hottest part of the garden.

Recommended
R. hirta forms a bristly mound of foliage and bears bright yellow, daisy-like flowers with brown centres that bloom from summer until the first frost. A wide variety of cultivars are available, including dwarf plants, double-flowered plants and plants with lime green rather than brown centres.

Perennial selections are also available.

Black-eyed Susan is a long-lasting vase flower. It makes a stunning display when combined with purple and burgundy flowers.

Also called: gloriosa daisy, annual rudbeckia, coneflower **Features:** colourful flowers **Flower colour:** yellow, orange, red, mahogany, brown or sometimes bicoloured; brown or green centres **Height:** 20–90 cm (8–36") or more **Spread:** 30–45 cm (12–18")

Calendula
Calendula

C. officinalis 'Apricot Surprise' (above), C. officinalis (below)

Calendula flowers, with their warm colours and saffron-like flavour, are popular kitchen herbs. Try them in a variety of dishes, including soups, stews, salads, baking, egg and cheese dishes or as a garnish.

Calendulas are bright and charming, and produce attractive flowers in warm colours all summer and fall.

Growing
Calendula prefers **full sun**. It likes cool weather and can withstand a moderate frost. The soil should be of **average fertility** and **well drained**. Deadhead to prolong blooming and keep plants looking neat. If plants fade in summer, cut them back to 10–15 cm (4–6") above the ground to promote new growth, or pull them up and seed new ones. Either method will produce a good fall display.

Tips
This informal plant looks attractive in borders and mixed into the vegetable patch. It can also be used in mixed planters. Calendula is a cold-hardy annual and often continues flowering, even through a layer of snow, until the ground freezes completely.

Recommended
C. officinalis is a vigorous, tough, upright plant that bears daisy-like, single or double flowers in a wide range of yellow and orange shades. Several cultivars are available.

Also called: pot marigold, English marigold **Features:** colourful flowers, long blooming period **Flower colour:** cream, yellow, gold, orange, apricot **Height:** 25–60 cm (10–24") **Spread:** 20–50 cm (8–20")

Coleus
Solenostemon (Coleus)

There is a coleus for everyone. With colours ranging from yellow, orange and red to green, deep maroon and rose, coleus variations are almost limitless.

Growing
Coleus prefers to grow in **light shade** or **partial shade,** but it tolerates full shade if the shade isn't too dense and full sun if the plants are watered regularly. The soil should be of **rich to average fertility, humus rich, moist** and **well drained**.

If you're growing plants from seed, place the seeds in a refrigerator for one or two days before planting them. They need light to germinate. Seedlings will be green at first, but leaf variegation will develop as the plants mature. Attractive specimens can be propagated from stem cuttings.

Tips
The bold, colourful foliage creates a dramatic look when the plants are grouped together as edging or in beds, borders or mixed containers. Coleus can also be grown indoors as a houseplant in a bright room.

Mixed cultivars (above & below)

Train your coleus to grow into a standard (tree) form by pinching the side branches off the central stalk as they grow. Once the plant reaches the desired height, pinch from the top and allow the plant to bush out to form a globe.

When flower buds develop, it is best to pinch them off because the plants tend to stretch out and look less attractive after they flower. Pinch plants regularly to encourage full and bushy growth.

Recommended
S. scutellarioides forms a bushy mound of foliage. The leaf edges range from slightly toothed to very ruffled. The leaves are usually multicoloured with shades ranging from pale greenish yellow to deep purple-black. Hundreds of cultivars are available, but many cannot be started from seed and are generally propagated from stem cuttings.

Features: brightly coloured foliage in varied shapes
Flower colour: light purple, grown as a foliage plant
Height: 15–90 cm (6–36") **Spread:** usually equal to height

Dusty Miller
Senecio

S. cineraria (above & below)

Dusty miller makes an artful addition to planters, window boxes and mixed borders where the soft, silvery grey, deeply lobed foliage makes a good backdrop for the brightly coloured flowers of other annuals.

Growing
Dusty miller prefers **full sun** but tolerates light shade. The soil should be of **average fertility** and **well drained**.

Mix dusty miller with geraniums, begonias or cockscombs to bring out the vibrant colours of those flowers, or interplant it with dark-foliaged annuals to create contrast.

Tips
This plant's soft, silvery, lacy leaves are its main feature. Dusty miller is used primarily as an edging plant, but it can also be planted in beds, borders and containers.

Pinch off any flowers that form before they bloom. They aren't showy and they steal energy that would otherwise go to producing more foliage.

Recommended
S. cineraria forms a mound of fuzzy, silvery grey, lobed or finely divided foliage. Many cultivars with impressive foliage colours and shapes have been developed. **'Cirrus'** has the most deeply dissected foliage.

Features: silvery foliage, neat habit **Flower colour:** yellow to cream, grown for silvery foliage **Height:** 30–60 cm (12–24") **Spread:** equal to height or slightly narrower

Fan Flower
Scaevola

Fan flower's intriguing one-sided flowers add flair to hanging baskets, planters and window boxes.

Growing

Fan flower grows well in **full sun** or **light shade**. The soil should be of **average fertility, moist** and **very well drained**. Although these plants are heat tolerant they should be watered regularly because they don't like to dry out completely. If plants become rangy and flowering slows, trim them back to encourage new growth and more flowers.

Tips

Fan flower is most often used in hanging baskets and containers, but it can also be planted along the tops of rock walls and in rock gardens where it will trail down. This plant makes an interesting addition to mixed borders and can be planted under shrubs, where the long, trailing stems will form an attractive groundcover and fill in the gaps between other plants.

S. aemula (above & below)

Recommended

S. aemula forms a mound of foliage from which trailing stems emerge. The fan-shaped flowers come in shades of purple, usually with white bases. The species is rarely grown because there are many improved cultivars, including white and bicoloured selections.

Given the right conditions, this Australian plant will form a cascading mass and will flower abundantly from spring to the first frost.

Features: unique flowers, trailing habit **Flower colour:** blue, purple, white **Height:** up to 20 cm (8") **Spread:** up to 90 cm (36") or more

Gazania
Gazania

G. *rigens* (above & below)

Few other flowers can rival gazania's vivid oranges, reds and yellows in the garden.

Growing

Gazania grows best in **full sun** but tolerates some shade. The soil should be of **poor to average fertility, sandy** and **well drained**. Gazania is drought tolerant and grows best when temperatures climb over 25° C (77° F). Flowers close on cloudy days, though some new selections bloom regardless of the weather.

Tips

Low-growing gazania makes an excellent groundcover in hot, dry sites and is also useful on exposed slopes, in mixed containers and as an edging in flowerbeds. It is a wonderful plant for a xeriscape or dry garden design.

Recommended

G. rigens forms a low basal rosette of lobed foliage. Large, daisy-like flowers with pointed petals are borne on strong stems above the plant. Many cultivars are available, including selections with silvery grey or variegated foliage and flowers with distinctive brown blotches at the petal bases.

Also called: African daisy, treasure flower
Features: colourful flowers **Flower colour:** red, orange, yellow, pink, cream **Height:** usually 15–20 cm (6–8"); may reach 30–45 cm (12–18") **Spread:** 20–30 cm (8–12")

Geranium
Pelargonium

Tough, predictable, sun-loving and drought-resistant, geraniums have earned their place as flowering favourites in the annual garden.

Growing
Geraniums prefer **full sun** but will tolerate partial shade, though they may not bloom as profusely. The soil should be **fertile** and **well drained**. Flowers should be snapped off and plants should be pinched back when they are planted.

Deadhead to keep geraniums blooming and looking neat. Remove flower clusters where they attach to the plant just before they are completely spent.

Tips
Geraniums are very popular annual plants, used in borders, beds, planters, hanging baskets and window boxes.

Recommended
P. x hortorum (zonal geranium) is a bushy plant with red, pink, purple, orange or white flowers and frequently banded or multi-coloured foliage. Many cultivars are available.

P. peltatum (ivy-leaved geranium) has thick, waxy leaves and a trailing habit. Many cultivars are available.

P. species and **cultivars** (scented geraniums, scented pelargoniums) is a large group of geraniums that have scented and often decorative variegated, deeply lobed or puckered leaves. Their fragrances include rose, mint, citrus, fruit, spice and chocolate.

P. peltatum (above & below)

Geraniums are tender perennials that are treated as annuals and can be kept indoors over winter in a bright room.

Features: colourful flowers, decorative or scented foliage, variable habits **Flower colour:** red, pink, violet, orange, salmon, white, purple **Height:** 20–60 cm (8–24") **Spread:** 15 cm–1.2 m (6"–4')

Heliotrope

Heliotropium

H. arborescens (above & below)

In addition to its sweet, vanilla-like scent, heliotrope has beautiful flowers that attract many kinds of butterflies.

Growing

Heliotrope grows best in full sun. The soil should be **fertile**, rich in **organic matter, moist** and **well drained**. Although over-watering will blacken the leaves and eventually kill heliotrope, this plant will be slow to recover if left to dry to the point of wilting. Heliotrope is sensitive to cold weather, so plant it out after all danger of frost has passed. Deadhead regularly.

Tips

Heliotrope is ideal for growing in containers or beds near windows and patios where the wonderful scent of the flowers can be enjoyed.

Recommended

H. arborescens is a low, bushy shrub that is treated as an annual. It grows 45–60 cm (18–24") tall with an equal spread. Large, scented clusters of purple, blue or white flowers are produced all summer. Some new cultivars are not as strongly scented as the species. **'Blue Wonder,'** however, was developed for its heavily scented, dark purple flowers on plants up to 40 cm (16") tall. **'Dwarf Marine'** ('Mini Marine') is a compact, bushy plant with fragrant, purple flowers that grows 20–30 cm (8–12") tall.

Also called: cherry pie plant **Features:** fragrant flowers, habit, foliage, attracts butterflies **Flower colour:** purple, blue, white **Height:** 20–60 cm (8–24") **Spread:** 30–60 cm (12–24")

Impatiens
Impatiens

Impatiens are the high-wattage darlings of the shade garden. They deliver masses of flowers in a wide variety of colours and are considered the most popular annual for shade gardens.

Growing
Impatiens do best in **partial shade** or **light shade** but will tolerate full shade. New Guinea impatiens tolerate sunny locations. The soil should be **fertile, humus rich, moist** and **well drained**.

Tips
Impatiens are known for their ability to grow and flower profusely even in shade. Mass plant them in beds, under trees, along shady fences or walls or in porch planters. They also look lovely in hanging baskets. New Guinea impatiens are grown as much for their leaf colour as for their flowers.

Recommended
I. hawkeri (New Guinea hybrids, New Guinea impatiens) has sun-tolerant flowers in shades of red, orange, pink, purple or white. The dark green to purple foliage is sometimes variegated, with a yellow stripe down the centre of each leaf.

I. walleriana (impatiens, busy Lizzie) flowers in shades of purple, red, burgundy, pink, yellow, salmon, orange, apricot and white and can be bicoloured. Dozens of cultivars are available.

I. walleriana (above), *I. hawkeri* (below)

The English named I. walleriana *"busy Lizzie" because it flowers continuously through the growing season. The name* impatiens *refers to the way the ripe seedpods burst when touched.*

Also called: busy Lizzie **Features:** colourful flowers, grows well in shade **Flower colour:** shades of purple, red, burgundy, pink, yellow, salmon, orange, apricot, white; also bicoloured with splashes, swirls or picotee edges
Height: 15–90 cm (6–36")
Spread: 30–60 cm (12–24")

Licorice Plant
Helichrysum

The silvery sheen of licorice plant is caused by a fine, soft pubescence on the leaves. Licorice plant will complement any other plant because silver is the ultimate blending colour.

Growing
Licorice plant prefers **full sun**. The soil should be of **poor to average fertility, neutral** or **alkaline** and **well drained**. Licorice plant wilts when the soil dries excessively but revives quickly once watered. If it outgrows its space, trim it back.

Tips
Licorice plant is a perennial grown as an annual that is prized for its foliage rather than its flowers. Include it in your hanging baskets, planters and window boxes to provide a soft, silvery backdrop for the colourful flowers of other plants. Licorice plant can also be used as a groundcover in beds, borders, rock gardens and along the tops of retaining walls.

H. petiolare cultivar (above), 'Limelight' (below)

H. thianschanium, *another species of licorice plant, has been recently introduced; it has a more upright habit and fine, narrow leaves. 'Icicles' is a popular cultivar.*

Recommended
H. petiolare is a branching, trailing plant with fuzzy, grey-green leaves. Cultivars are more common than the species and include varieties with lime green, silver or variegated leaves, as well as a selection with tiny leaves.

Features: trailing or upright habit; colourful, fuzzy foliage **Flower colour:** plant grown for foliage **Height:** 50 cm (20") **Spread:** 90 cm (36") or more

Love-in-a-Mist
Nigella

N. damascena (above & below)

*L*ove-in-a-mist's ferny foliage and delicate blue flowers blend beautifully with most plants. It has a tendency to self-sow and may show up in unexpected spots in your garden for years to come.

Growing

Love-in-a-mist prefers **full sun**. The soil should be of **average fertility, light** and **well drained**.

Direct sow seeds at two-week intervals from spring to early June to prolong the blooming period. These plants will self-seed, but they resent being disturbed. Seedlings should be transplanted carefully, if at all.

Tips

This attractive, airy plant is often used in mixed beds and borders. The unusual flowers appear to float above the delicate foliage. Blooming may be slow and the plants may die back if the weather gets too hot in summer. Cut plants back to rejuvenate them.

The stems of this plant can be floppy and may benefit from being staked with twiggy branches. Poke the branches into the dirt around the plant when it is young, and the plant will grow between the twigs.

Recommended

N. damascena forms a loose mound of finely divided foliage. Cultivars are available in a wide variety of flower colours and forms, including bicoloured and double flowers.

Also called: devil-in-a-bush **Features:** feathery foliage, exotic flowers, interesting seed pods **Flower colour:** blue, white, pink, purple **Height:** 40–60 cm (16–24") **Spread:** 20–30 cm (8–12")

Marigold
Tagetes

T. tenuifolia (above), *T. patula* (below)

Studies show that the marigold's natural oils suppress nematodes, but it is debatable whether the plant's presence in the garden is enough to deter other insects.

From the large, exotic, ruffled flowers of African marigold to the tiny flowers on the low-growing signet marigold, this plant's warm colours add a festive touch to the garden.

Growing

Marigolds grow best in **full sun**. The soil should be of **average fertility** and **well drained**. These plants are drought tolerant and hold up well in windy, rainy weather. Sow seed directly or start early and transplant seedlings into the garden after the risk of frost has passed. Deadhead to prolong blooming and to keep plants tidy.

Tips

Mass planted or mixed with other plants, marigolds make a vibrant addition to beds, borders and container gardens. These plants will thrive in the hottest, driest parts of your garden.

Recommended

T. erecta (African marigold, American marigold, Aztec marigold) has the largest plants with the biggest flowers; low-growing *T. patula* (French marigold) has a wide range of flower colours; *T. tenuifolia* (signet marigold) has become more popular recently because of its feathery foliage and small, dainty, edible flowers; *T.* **Triploid Hybrids** (triploid marigold) have been developed by crossing French and African marigolds, thus producing plants with huge flowers and compact growth. There are many cultivars available for all the above selections.

Features: brightly coloured, scented flowers; scented foliage **Flower colour:** yellow, red, orange, mahogany, brown, gold, cream, bicoloured **Height:** 15–90 cm (6–36") **Spread:** 30–60 cm (12–24")

Million Bells
Calibrachoa

*M*illion bells is a charming plant that, given the right conditions, blooms continually during the growing season.

Growing
Million bells prefers **full sun**. The soil should be **fertile, moist** and **well drained**. Although it prefers to be watered regularly, million bells is fairly drought resistant once established.

Tips
A popular choice for planters and hanging baskets, million bells also looks attractive in beds and borders. It grows all summer and into fall, and needs plenty of room to spread or it will overtake other flowers. Pinch back to keep plants compact.

Recommended
Calibrachoa **hybrids** have a dense, trailing habit. They bear small flowers that look like petunias but tolerate humid conditions better than petunias. Cultivars are available in a wide range of flower colours.

'Trailing Blue' (above), 'Trailing Pink' (below)

Million bells blooms well into autumn. It becomes hardier over summer and as the weather cools.

Also called: calibrachoa, trailing petunia **Features:** colourful flowers, trailing habit **Flower colour:** pink, purple, yellow, red-orange, copper, gold, white, blue **Height:** 15–30 cm (6–12") **Spread:** up to 60 cm (24")

Nasturtium
Tropaeolum

T. majus (above), T. m. Alaska Mixed (below)

Nasturtium leaves, flower buds and flowers are edible. They add a peppery flavour to gourmet salads and can serve as a decorative garnish.

These fast-growing, brightly coloured flowers are easy to grow, making them popular with beginners and experienced gardeners alike.

Growing
Nasturtiums prefer **full sun** but tolerate light shade. The soil should be of **poor to average fertility, light, moist** and **well drained**. Soil that is too rich or has too much nitrogen fertilizer will result in lots of leaves and very few flowers. Let the soil drain completely between waterings. Sow directly in the garden once the danger of frost has passed. Plants can be started early in peat pots to avoid disturbing the roots when transplanting.

Tips
Nasturtiums are used in beds, borders, containers and hanging baskets and on sloped banks. The climbing varieties are grown up trellises or over rock walls and places that need concealing. These plants thrive in poor, cool locations.

Recommended
T. majus has a trailing habit, but many of its cultivars have bushier, more refined habits. Cultivars also offer differing flower colours and variegated foliage.

Features: brightly coloured flowers, attractive leaves, edible leaves and flowers, varied habits **Flower colour:** red, orange, yellow, burgundy, pink, cream, gold, white or bicoloured **Height:** 30–45 cm (12–18") for dwarf varieties; up to 3 m (10') for trailing or climbing varieties **Spread:** equal to height

Nicotiana
Nicotiana

Nicotianas were originally cultivated for their wonderful flower fragrance, a feature that, in some cases, was lost when hybridizers focused on expanding the selection of flower colours. Fragrant varieties are, however, still available.

Growing

Nicotianas grow equally well in **full sun, light shade** or **partial shade**. The soil should be **fertile, high in organic matter, moist** and **well drained**. Nicotianas tolerate light fall frosts. They tend to self-seed and young seedlings can be transplanted as desired.

Tips

Nicotianas delicately fill empty spaces, and are popular choices for beds and borders, edge plantings and dramatic backdrops. All nicotianas do well in containers, but the dwarf varieties are best suited to this application. Do not plant nicotianas near tomatoes because, as members of the same plant family, they share a vulnerability to many of the same diseases.

Recommended

N. langsdorfii bears delicate, airy clusters of lime green, trumpet-shaped flowers on plants 90 cm–1.5 m (3–5') tall.

N. x sanderae (*N. alata* x *N. forgetiana*) is a hybrid from which many bushy cultivars with showy, brightly coloured flowers have been developed.

N. sylvestris grows 1.2 m (4') tall or more, with bright green leaves and terminal clusters of pendulous, fragrant, white flowers.

N. x sanderae (above & below)

Nicotiana flowers are most fragrant in the evening; N. sylvestris *has the most captivating scent.*

Also called: flowering tobacco plant
Features: fragrant or colourful flowers
Flower colour: red, pink, green, yellow, white, purple **Height:** 30 cm–1.5 m (12–60")
Spread: 30 cm (12")

Petunia
Petunia

Multiflora petunia (above & below)

For speedy growth, prolific blooming, bright colours and ease of care, petunias are hard to beat. They remain one of the most popular bedding plants.

Growing
Petunias prefer **full sun** but tolerate light shade. The soil should be of **average to rich fertility, light, sandy** and **well drained**. Pinch halfway back in mid-summer to keep plants bushy and to encourage new growth and flowers.

Tips
Among the many available petunias, choose the ones best suited to your space and purpose—beds, borders, edging, groundcovers, containers or hanging baskets. You are sure to find a petunia that suits your needs.

Recommended
P. x *hybrida* is a large group of popular, sun-loving annuals whose cultivars fall into three categories: **grandifloras** have the largest flowers in the widest range of colours, but they can be damaged by rain; **multifloras** bear more flowers that are smaller and less easily damaged by heavy rain; **millifloras** have the smallest flowers in the narrowest range of colours, but this type is the most prolific and least likely to be damaged by heavy rain.

Features: colourful, single to fully double flowers; versatile plants **Flower colour:** many shades of pink, purple, red, mauve, white, yellow, coral, blue; solid, bicoloured, striped, swirled or picotee edged. **Height:** 15–45 cm (6–18") **Spread:** 30–60 cm (12–24") or wider

Phormium
Phormium

*T*hese bold and impressive plants create quite an impact. They will become the focal point of any planting.

Growing
Phormium grows best in **full sun**. Soil should be **fertile, moist** and **well drained**. These plants are heavy feeders, and can be overwintered indoors in a bright, cool, but frost-free location.

Tips
Use phormium in beds and borders or in container plantings near entryways and walkways where their vertical form can add architectural appeal.

Recommended
There is a wide selection of available species, hybrids and cultivars. These plants have broad, strap-shaped, colourful foliage. Many plants mature at over 1.8 m (6') tall, with equal spreads, but when grown as annuals, they rarely get this big. Dwarf cultivars that mature to about 60 cm (24") tall are also available.

P. cookianum 'Sundowner' (above), *P. tenax* cultivar (below)

Phormiums are tender perennials that are grown as annuals. As their breeding develops, more new and exciting selections will become available.

Also called: New Zealand flax
Features: colourful green, black, red or yellow, often multicoloured and striped foliage
Flower colour: grown for foliage
Height: 60 cm–1.8 cm (2–6')
Spread: 60 cm–1.8 cm (2–6')

Poppy
Papaver

P. nudicaule (above), P. orientale (below)

Be careful when weeding around faded summer plants so that you don't weed out late-summer poppy seedlings.

Poppies look like they were meant to grow in groups. Swaying in a breeze atop often-curving stems, the flowers seem to be engaged in lively conversation.

Growing

Poppies grow best in **full sun**. The soil should be **fertile** and **sandy** with lots of **organic matter** mixed in. **Good drainage** is essential. Direct sow every two weeks in spring, or sow in fall for earlier spring blooms. Mix the tiny seeds with fine sand for even sowing. Do not cover—the seeds need light for germination. Deadhead to prolong blooming.

Tips

Poppies work well in mixed borders. They will empty spaces early in the season, then die back over the summer, leaving room for slower plants to fill. Poppies can also be used in rock gardens, and the cut flowers look good in fresh arrangements.

Recommended

P. nudicaule (Iceland poppy) bears red, orange, yellow, pink or white flowers in spring and early summer.

P. orientale (Oriental poppy) is a perennial rather than an annual poppy, but because the plants tend to die back over the summer, they are sometimes mistaken for annuals. Oriental poppies are renowned for their large, bright red, dark-centered, early-summer flowers.

P. rhoeas (Flanders poppy, field poppy, corn poppy) forms a basal rosette of foliage. Its flowers, in a wide range of colours, are borne on long stems.

Features: brightly coloured flowers **Flower colour:** red, pink, white, purple, yellow, orange **Height:** 60–90 cm (24–36") **Spread:** 30 cm (12")

Portulaca
Portulaca

For a brilliant show in the hottest, driest, most sun-baked and neglected area of the garden, you can't go wrong with portulaca.

Growing
Portulaca requires **full sun**. The soil should be of **poor fertility, sandy** and **well drained**. To ensure that your plants grow where you want them, start seed indoors. If you sow directly outdoors, the tiny seeds may get washed away by rain and the self-seeding plants will pop up in unexpected places. This often occurs, but new seedlings can be transplanted as needed. Weed out the rest.

Tips
Portulaca is the ideal plant for garden spots that don't get enough water, such as under the eaves of a house or in dry, rocky, exposed areas along pathways and in rock walls. It is also an ideal plant for people who like hanging baskets on the front porch but who sometimes neglect to water.

Recommended
P. grandiflora forms a bushy mound of succulent foliage. It bears delicate, silky, rose-like, single or double flowers profusely all summer. Many cultivars are available, including those with flowers that stay open on cloudy days.

P. grandiflora (above & below)

These low-maintenance plants can be placed close together and allowed to intertwine for an interesting and attractive effect.

Also called: moss rose, purslane
Features: colourful, drought- and heat-resistant flowers **Flower colour:** red, pink, yellow, white, purple, orange, peach
Height: 10–20 cm (4–8") **Spread:** 15–30 cm (6–12") or wider

Salvia
Salvia

S. *splendens* with S. *farinacea* in background (above), S. *viridis* (below)

The salvias, with their attractive and varied forms, have something to offer every style of garden.

Growing
All salvia plants prefer **full sun** but tolerate light shade. The soil should be **moist, well drained** and of **average to rich fertility** with lots of **organic matter**.

Tips
Salvias look good grouped in beds, borders and containers. The flowers are long lasting and make good cut flowers for arrangements.

To keep plants producing flowers, water often and fertilize monthly.

Recommended
S. argentea (silver sage) is grown for its large, fuzzy, silvery leaves. ***S. coccinea*** (Texas sage) is a bushy, upright plant that bears whorled spikes of white, pink, blue or purple flowers. ***S. farinacea*** (mealy cup sage, blue sage) has bright blue flowers clustered along stems powdered with silver. Cultivars are available. ***S. splendens*** (salvia, scarlet sage) is grown for its spikes of bright red, tubular flowers. Recently, cultivars have become available in white, pink, purple and orange. ***S. viridis*** (*S. horminium*; annual clary sage) is grown for its showy and colourful pink, purple, blue or white wing-like bracts, rather than its flowers.

Also called: sage **Features:** colourful summer flowers, attractive foliage **Flower colour:** red, blue, purple, burgundy, pink, orange, salmon, yellow, cream, white or bicoloured **Height:** 20 cm–1.2 m (8"–4') **Spread:** 20 cm–1.2 m (8"–4')

Sunflower
Helianthus

There are many sunflower options and each one adds cheerful charm to any location. I have never seen a sunflower I didn't like.

Growing
Sunflower grows best in **full sun**. The soil should be of **average fertility, humus rich, moist** and **well drained**. Successive plantings from spring to early summer will prolong the blooming period.

The annual sunflower is an excellent plant for a child's garden. The seeds are big and easy to handle, and they germinate quickly. The plants grow continually upward, and their progress can be measured until the flower finally appears on top.

Tips
Lower-growing varieties can be used in beds, borders and containers. Tall varieties work well at the back of borders and make good screens and temporary hedges. The tallest varieties may need staking.

H. annuus 'Teddy Bear' (above), a typical cultivar (below)

Recommended
H. annuus (common sunflower) has attractive cultivars in a wide range of heights, with single stems or branching habits. Flowers come in a variety of colours, in single to fully double forms.

Features: late-summer flowers, edible seeds
Flower colour: most commonly yellow but also orange, red, brown, cream or bicoloured; typically with brown, purple or rusty red centres. **Height:** dwarf varieties, 40 cm (16"); giants up to 4.5 m (15')
Spread: 30–60 cm (12–24")

Sweet Alyssum
Lobularia

L. maritima cultivars (above & below)

Sweet alyssum is excellent for creating soft edges, and it self-seeds, popping up along pathways and between stones late in the season to give summer a sweet sendoff.

Growing

Sweet alyssum prefers **full sun** but tolerates light shade. **Well-drained** soil of **average fertility** is preferred, but poor soil is tolerated. Sweet alyssum may die back a bit during the heat and humidity of summer.

Leave alyssum plants out all winter. In spring, remove the previous year's growth to expose self-sown seedlings below.

Trim this plant back and water it periodically to encourage new growth and more flowers when the weather cools.

Tips

Sweet alyssum creeps around rock gardens, billows over rock walls and fills the edges of beds and containers. It can be seeded into cracks and crevices of walkways and between patio stones. Once established, it readily reseeds. It is also good for filling in spaces between taller plants in borders and mixed containers.

Recommended

L. maritima forms a low, spreading mound of foliage. The entire plant appears to be covered in tiny, fragrant blossoms when in full flower. Cultivars with flowers in a wide range of colours are available.

Features: fragrant flowers **Flower colour:** pink, purple, yellow, salmon, white **Height:** 8–30 cm (3–12") **Spread:** 15–60 cm (6–24")

Sweet Potato Vine

Ipomoea

I. batatas 'Blackie' (above), *I. b.* 'Marguerite' (below)

This vigorous rambling plant with lime green, purple, coppery bronze or green, pink and cream variegated leaves makes a dramatic impact unsurpassed by any other annual plant.

Growing

Grow sweet potato vine in **full sun**, or in **partial shade** for variegated selections. Any type of soil will do, but an **average to fertile, light, well-drained** soil is preferred.

Tips

Sweet potato vine makes a great addition to mixed planters, window boxes and hanging baskets. It will cascade over the top of a retaining wall. The edible tubers that form on the roots can break wooden window boxes if placed too close together.

Recommended

I. batatas (sweet potato vine) is a scrambling, trailing plant grown for its attractive foliage. Several cultivars are available, including **'Blackie,'** with purple-black, deeply lobed foliage; **'Marguerite,'** with yellow-green foliage; and **'Tricolour,'** with green, white and pink variegated foliage.

Morning glory (Ipomoea tricolour) is a closely related twining vine that produces showy, funnel-shaped flowers in shades of blue and pink.

Features: decorative foliage **Flower colour:** grown for foliage **Height:** about 30 cm (12") **Spread:** up to 3 m (10')

Verbena
Verbena

V. bonariensis (above), *V. x hybrida* (below)

Verbenas offer butterflies a banquet. These winged visitors include tiger swallowtails, silver-spotted skippers, great spangled fritillaries and painted ladies.

Growing
Verbenas grow best in **full sun**. The soil should be **fertile** and **very well drained**. These plants are drought and heat tolerant. Pinch back the young plants for bushy growth. Deadhead garden verbenas to encourage blooming and other verbenas to reduce self-seeding.

Tips
Use verbenas on rock walls and in beds, borders, rock gardens, containers, hanging baskets and window boxes. Garden verbenas make good substitutes for ivy-leaved geranium where the sun is hot and where a roof overhang keeps the mildew-prone verbenas dry.

Recommended
V. bonariensis (Brazilian verbena) forms a low clump of foliage on which tall, stiff stems bear clusters of small, purple flowers.

V. x hybrida (garden verbena) is a bushy plant with fern-like leaves and an upright or spreading form. It bears clusters of small flowers in a wide range of colours. Cultivars are available.

V. rigida (vervain, rigid verbena) is similar in flower and form to *V. bonariensis*, but it is a smaller plant.

Also called: garden verbena **Features:** summer flowers **Flower colour:** red, pink, purple, blue, yellow, scarlet, silver, peach or white; some have white centres **Height:** 20 cm–1.2 m (8"–4') **Spread:** 30–90 cm (12-36")

Ajuga
Ajuga

A. reptans cultivar (above), *A. r.* 'Burgundy Glow' (below)

Often labelled a rampant runner, ajuga grows best where it can roam freely without competition.

Growing

Ajugas develop the best leaf colour in **partial or light shade**, but they tolerate full shade. The leaves may become scorched when exposed to too much sun. Any **well-drained** soil is suitable. Divide these vigorous plants any time during the growing season.

Remove any new growth or seedlings that don't show the hybrid leaf colouring.

Tips

Ajugas make excellent groundcovers for difficult sites, such as exposed slopes and dense shade. They also look attractive in shrub borders, where their dense growth prevents the spread of all but the most tenacious weeds.

Recommended

A. genevensis (Geneva bugleweed) is an upright, noninvasive species that bears blue, white or pink spring flowers.

A. pyramidalis 'Metallica Crispa' (upright bugleweed) is a very slow-growing plant with metallic bronzy brown, crinkly foliage and violet blue flowers.

A. reptans (common bugleweed) is a low, quick-spreading groundcover. Its many cultivars are more popular than the species because of their colourful, often variegated foliage.

Also called: bugleweed Features: late-spring to early-summer flowers, colourful foliage Flower colour: purple, blue, pink, white; grown for decorative foliage Height: 8–30 cm (3–12") Spread: 15–90 cm (6–36") Hardiness: zones 3–8

Artemisia

Artemisia

A. ludoviciana 'Silver Queen' (above), *A. l.* 'Valerie Finnis' (below)

Most of the artemisias are valued for their silvery foliage rather than their insignificant flowers. Silver is the ultimate blending colour in the garden because it enhances every hue combined with it.

Growing

Artemisias grow best in **full sun**. The soil should be of **low to average fertility** and **well drained**. These plants dislike wet, humid conditions.

Tips

Use artemisias in border plantings. Smaller species and dwarf cultivars can be included in rock gardens. Their silvery grey foliage makes them good backdrop plants for brightly coloured flowers. They are also useful for filling in spaces between other plants.

Recommended

A. ludoviciana (white sage, silver sage) is an upright, clump-forming plant with silvery white foliage. The species is not grown as often as cultivars such as '**Silver King,**' '**Silver Queen**' and '**Valerie Finnis.**' (Zones 4–8)

A. x '**Powis Castle**' is a compact, mounding, shrubby plant with feathery, silvery grey foliage. This hybrid is reliably hardy to zone 6, but it can also grow in colder regions with winter protection and a sheltered site.

A. schmidtiana (silvermound artemisia) is a low, dense, mound-forming perennial with feathery, hairy, silvery grey foliage. '**Nana**' (dwarf silvermound) is very compact and grows only half the size of the species.

Also called: wormwood, sage, white sage
Features: silvery grey, feathery or deeply lobed foliage **Flower colour:** plant grown for foliage **Height:** 15–90 cm (6–36") **Spread:** 30–90 cm (12–36") **Hardiness:** zones 3–8

Aster

Aster

Among the final plants to bloom before the snow flies, asters often provide a last meal for migrating butterflies. Purple and pink asters make a nice contrast to the yellow-flowered perennials common in the late-summer garden.

Growing
Asters grow best in **full sun**. The soil should be **fertile**, **moist** and **well drained**. Pinch or shear these plants back in early summer to promote dense growth and reduce disease problems. Mulch in winter to protect plants from temperature fluctuations. Divide every two to three years to maintain vigour and to control spread.

Tips
Use asters in the middle of borders and in cottage gardens, or naturalize them in wild gardens.

Recommended
Some aster species have recently been reclassified under the genus *Symphyotrichum*. You may see both names at garden centres.

A. novae-angliae (New England aster, Michaelmas daisy) is an upright, spreading, clump-forming perennial that bears yellow-centred, purple flowers. Many cultivars with pink, lavender, purple or red flowers are available.

A. novi-belgii (New York aster, Michaelmas daisy) is a dense, upright, clumpforming perennial with purple flowers. Cultivars with flowers in other colours are available.

A. novi-belgii (above & below)

Tall asters may require staking to prevent them from flopping over.

Features: late-summer to mid-autumn flowers **Flower colour:** red, white, blue, purple, lavender, pink; often with yellow centres **Height:** 25 cm–1.5 m (10"–5') **Spread:** 45–90 cm (18–36") **Hardiness:** zones 3–8

Astilbe
Astilbe

A. x arendsii (above), *A. x arendsii* 'Bressingham Beauty' (below)

Astilbes are beacons in the shade. Their high-impact flowers will brighten any gloomy section of your garden.

Growing
Astilbes grow best in **light shade** or **partial shade** and tolerate full shade, though they will not flower as much in full shade. If mulched, they will even tolerate full sun, though leaf scorch may occur during hot summers. The soil should be **fertile, humus rich, acidic, moist** and **well drained**. Although they appreciate moist soil, they don't like standing water.

Astilbes should be divided every three years or so to maintain plant vigour. Root masses may lift out of the soil as they mature. Lift, divide and replant to invigorate plants if this happens.

Tips
Astilbes are versatile perennials that can be grown near the edges of bog gardens and ponds, in woodland gardens and in shaded borders.

Recommended
A. x *arendsii* (astilbe, false spirea, hybrid astilbe) is the largest group of hybrids, with many available cultivars.

A. chinensis (Chinese astilbe) is a dense, vigorous, spreading perennial with lacy foliage. It tolerates dry soil better than other astilbe species. Many cultivars are available.

A. japonica (Japanese astilbe) is a compact, clump-forming perennial. Cultivars are preferred over the species

Features: summer flowers, attractive foliage
Flower colour: white, pink, purple, peach, red
Height: 25 cm–1.2 m (10"–4') **Spread:** 20–90 cm (8–36") **Hardiness:** zones 3–8

Barrenwort
Epimedium

ong lived and low maintenance with attractive, heart-shaped, often colourful foliage and delicate sprays of orchid-like flowers, this plant is a woodland garden favourite.

Growing
Barrenwort grows best in **light shade** or **partial shade** but tolerates full shade. Soil should be **average to fertile, humus rich** and **moist**, though plants are fairly drought tolerant once established. Cut back the foliage, especially if it's tattered, before new growth begins in spring.

Tips
These spring-blooming plants are a popular addition to shade and woodland gardens, as accent plants or groundcovers. They can be planted under taller, shade-providing plants in beds and borders as well as in moist, pondside plantings. Barrenwort can be slow to establish, but it's worth the wait.

Recommended
Many species, hybrids and cultivars are grown for their attractive foliage and spring flowers. Plants may be clump forming or spreading in habit. *E.* x *cantabrigiense* is a clump-forming plant with dark green leaves and coppery orange flowers touched with red. *E. grandiflorum* is also a clump-forming plant. Its cultivars have large, delicate, creamy white to dark pink flowers. *E.* x *perralchium* 'Frohnleiten' is a compact, spreading plant with bright yellow flowers and reddish green foliage that persists into winter. *E.* x *rubrum*, a low-spreading plant with small, wine- and cream-coloured flowers, is one of the most popular groundcover selections.

E. x *rubrum* (above & below)

Single barrenwort plants add an elegant accent to the garden; large groups make a dramatic display.

Also called: epimedium, bishop's hat
Features: spring flowers, foliage, habit **Flower colour:** yellow, orange, cream, white, pink, red, purple **Height:** 15–45 cm (6–18") **Spread:** 30–60 cm (12–24") **Hardiness:** zones 4–8

Bellflower

Campanula

C. persicifolia (above), C. carpatica 'White Clips' (below)

⟨T⟩hanks to their wide range of heights and habits, it is possible to put bell-flowers almost anywhere in the garden.

Growing
Bellflowers grow well in **full sun** or **light shade**. The soil should be of **average to high fertility** and **well drained**. These plants appreciate a mulch to keep their roots cool and moist in summer and protected in winter, particularly if snow cover is inconsistent. Deadhead to prolong blooming.

Tips
Plant upright and mounding bellflowers in borders and cottage gardens. Use low, spreading and trailing bellflowers in rock gardens and on rock walls. You can also edge beds with the low-growing varieties.

Recommended
C. x **'Birch Hybrid'** (dwarf bellflower) is a low-growing and trailing plant. It bears light blue to mauve flowers in summer.

C. carpatica (Carpathian bellflower, Carpathian harebell) is a spreading, mounding perennial that bears blue, white or purple flowers in summer. Several cultivars are available.

C. glomerata (clustered bellflower) forms a clump of upright stems and bears clusters of purple, blue or white flowers throughout most of the summer.

C. persicifolia (peach-leaf bellflower) is an upright perennial that self-seeds and bears white, blue or purple flowers from early to mid-summer.

C. poscharskyana (Serbian bellflower) is a trailing perennial that likes to wind its way around other plants. It bears light violet blue flowers in summer and early autumn.

Also called: campanula **Features:** spring, summer or autumn flowers; varied growing habits **Flower colour:** blue, white, purple, pink **Height:** 10 cm–1.8 m (4"–6') **Spread:** 30–90 cm (12–36") **Hardiness:** zones 3–7

Blazing Star
Liatris

L. spicata 'Kobold' (above), *L. spicata* (below)

Blazing star is an outstanding cut flower with fuzzy, spiked blossoms above grass-like foliage. This native wildflower is an excellent plant for attracting butterflies to the garden.

Growing

Blazing star prefers **full sun**. The soil should be of **average fertility, sandy** and **humus rich**. Water well during the growing season, but don't allow the plants to stand in water during cool weather. Mulch during summer to prevent moisture loss. Established plants are quite drought tolerant.

Trim off the spent flower spikes to promote a longer blooming period and to keep blazing star looking tidy. Spikes can be left on the plant toward the end of the flowering season for winter interest. They will self-seed, but seedlings may not be identical to the parent plants.

Tips

Use this plant in borders and meadow plantings where the tall flowering spikes can create a striking contrast with other perennials and shrubs. Plant in a location that has good drainage to avoid root rot in winter. Blazing star grows well in planters.

Recommended

L. spicata is a clump-forming, erect plant with pinkish purple or white flowers. Several cultivars are available.

Also called: gayfeather **Features:** summer flowers, grass-like foliage **Flower colour:** purple, white **Height:** 45–90 cm (18–36") **Spread:** 45–60 cm (18–24") **Hardiness:** zones 3–8

Bleeding Heart

Dicentra

D. formosa (above), D. spectabilis (below)

Tucked away in a shady spot, this lovely plant appears in spring and fills the garden with fresh promise.

Growing

Bleeding hearts prefer **light shade** but tolerate partial or full shade. The soil should be **humus rich, moist** and **well drained**. Very dry summer conditions cause the plants to die back, though they will revive in autumn or the following spring. Bleeding hearts must remain moist while blooming in order to prolong the flowering period. Regular watering will keep the flowers coming until mid-summer.

Tips

Bleeding hearts can be naturalized in a woodland garden or grown in a border or rock garden. They make excellent early-season specimen plants and do well near ponds or streams.

All bleeding hearts contain toxic alkaloids, and some people develop allergic skin reactions from contact with these plants.

Recommended

D. eximia (fringed bleeding heart) forms a loose, mounded clump of lacy, fern-like, blue-green foliage that rarely goes dormant in summer. It bears pink or white flowers in spring and sporadically over summer.

D. formosa (western bleeding heart) is a low-growing, wide-spreading plant with pink flowers that fade to white as they mature. The most drought tolerant of the bleeding hearts, it is the most likely to continue flowering all summer.

D. spectabilis (common bleeding heart, Japanese bleeding heart) forms a large, elegant mound that usually goes dormant during hot weather if not watered. It bears flowers with white inner petals and pink outer petals. Several cultivars are available, including **'Pantaloons,'** an excellent white-flowered selection.

Features: spring and summer flowers, attractive foliage **Flower colour:** pink, white, red, purple **Height:** 30 cm–1.2 m (12"–4') **Spread:** 30–90 cm (12–36") **Hardiness:** zones 3–8

Bugbane
Cimicifuga

Bugbanes take a few years to become established, but once they settle in, they will display fragrant flowers above decorative foliage, making them worth the wait.

Growing
Bugbanes grow best in **partial or light shade**. The soil should be **fertile, humus rich** and **moist**. The plants may require support from a peony hoop. Bugbanes spread by rhizomes; small pieces of root can be carefully unearthed and replanted in spring if more plants are desired.

Tips
Bugbanes make attractive additions to an open woodland garden, shaded border or pondside planting. The bronze- and purple-leaved cultivars create a stunning contrast. Bugbanes don't compete well with tree roots or other plants that have vigorous roots. They are worth growing close to the house because the late-season flowers are wonderfully fragrant.

Recommended
C. racemosa (black snakeroot) is a clump-forming perennial with long-stemmed spikes of fragrant, creamy white flowers.

C. simplex (Kamchatka bugbane) is a clump-forming perennial with fragrant, bottlebrush-like spikes of flowers. Several ornamental cultivars are available, including those with bronze or purple foliage in the **Atropurpurea** group, such as **'Brunette'** and **'Hillside Black Beauty.'**

C. simplex cultivar (above), *C. racemosa* (below)

C. racemosa *is also known as black cohosh, and its rhizomes are used in herbal medicine.*

Also called: snakeroot, actaea **Features:** fragrant, late-summer and autumn flowers, some with bronze or purple foliage **Flower colour:** white, cream, pink **Height:** 90 cm–2.4 m (3–8') **Spread:** 60 cm (2') **Hardiness:** zones 3–8

Cardoon
Cynara

Big, bold and beautiful, this unique and architectural plant demands attention in the garden.

Growing
Cardoon grows best in full sun. Soil should be **very fertile** and **well drained**; these plants are heavy feeders. Ensure the location is sheltered from the wind. Flowers will only occur on plants that are successfully overwintered. In zone 6, Ontario's warmest region, a heavy winter mulch is required; in colder areas plants may be overwintered in a cold but frost-free location.

Tips
These striking plants can be included at the back of borders, planted singly or grouped together to form an impressive focal point in the garden. They create a striking display in a decorative urn.

Recommended
C. cardunculus, a clump-forming tender perennial, doesn't flower until August of its second year. It has silvery blue, thistle-like foliage and purple flowers. Flowers are produced from summer to fall and make interesting additions to fresh and dried arrangements.

C. cardunculus (above & below)

The closely related Cynara scolymus *produces edible flowerheads commonly known as artichokes.*

Features: foliage, flowers, habit
Flower colour: dark purple
Height: 1.5 m (5')
Spread: 1.2 m (4')
Hardiness: zones 6–8

Columbine
Aquilegia

*D*elicate and beautiful columbines add a touch of simple elegance to any garden. Blooming from spring through mid-summer, these long-lasting flowers herald the passing of cool spring weather and the arrival of summer.

Growing
Columbines grow well in **light shade or partial shade**. They prefer soil that is **fertile, moist** and **well drained**, but they adapt to most soil conditions. Division is not required but can be done to propagate desirable plants. Divided plants may take awhile to recover because columbines dislike having their roots disturbed.

Tips
Use columbines in rock gardens, formal or casual borders and naturalized or woodland gardens. Place them where other plants can hide their foliage as the columbines die back over the summer.

If leaf miners are a problem, cut the foliage back once flowering is complete and new foliage will fill in.

Recommended
A. canadensis (wild columbine, Canada columbine) is a native plant that is common in woodlands and fields. It bears yellow flowers with red spurs.

A. x *hybrida* (*A.* x *cultorum*, hybrid columbine) forms mounds of delicate foliage and has exceptional flowers. Many hybrids have been developed with showy flowers in a wide range of colours.

A. canadensis (above), A. x hybrida (below)

A. vulgaris (European columbine, common columbine) has been used to develop many hybrids and cultivars with flowers in a variety of colours and forms, including double-flowered cultivars that look like frilly dahlias.

Features: spring and summer flowers, attractive foliage
Flower colour: red, yellow, pink, purple, blue, white; colour of spurs often differs from that of the petals
Height: 45–90 cm (18–36") **Spread:** 30–60 cm (12–24") **Hardiness:** zones 3–8

Daylily
Hemerocallis

'Dewey Roquemore' (above), 'Bonanza' (below)

Daylilies were first cultivated 2500 years ago and have appeared in Chinese literature since 1000 BC.

The daylily's adaptability and durability combined with its variety in colour, blooming period, size and texture explain this perennial's popularity.

Growing

Daylilies grow in any light from **full sun to full shade**. The deeper the shade, the fewer flowers will be produced. The soil should be **fertile, moist** and **well drained**, but these plants adapt to most conditions and are hard to kill once established. Divide every two to three years to keep plants vigorous and to propagate them. They can, however, be left indefinitely without dividing.

Tips

Plant daylilies alone or group them in borders, on banks and in ditches to control erosion. They can be naturalized in woodland or meadow gardens. Small varieties look nice in planters and rock gardens.

Deadhead to prolong the blooming period. Be careful when deadheading purple-flowered daylilies because the sap can stain fingers and clothes.

Recommended

Daylilies come in an almost infinite number of forms, sizes and colours in a range of species, hybrids and cultivars. See your local garden centre or daylily grower to find out what's available and most suitable for your garden.

Features: spring and summer flowers, grass-like foliage **Flower colour:** every colour except blue and pure white **Height:** 30 cm–1.2 m (12"–4') **Spread:** 30 cm–1.2 m (12"–4') **Hardiness:** zones 2–8

Dead Nettle

Lamium

These attractive, low-growing plants have striped, dotted or banded silver and green foliage that adds a bright shimmer to the shade garden. Dead nettles are fabulous groundcovers that thrive on only the barest necessities.

Growing

Dead nettles prefer **partial to light shade**. They tolerate full sun but may become leggy. The soil should be of **average fertility, humus rich, moist** and **well drained**. The more fertile the soil, the more vigorously the plants will grow. These plants are drought tolerant when grown in the shade but can develop bare patches if the soil is allowed to dry out for extended periods. Divide and replant in autumn if bare spots become unsightly.

Dead nettles remain more compact if sheared back after flowering. If they remain green over winter, shear them back in early spring to promote the growth of fresh new shoots.

Tips

These plants make useful groundcovers for woodland or shade gardens. They also work well under shrubs in a border, where the dead nettles help keep weeds down.

L. maculatum 'Limelight' (above), *L. m.* 'Beacon Silver' (below)

Recommended

L. galeobdolon (*Lamiastrum galeobdolon*, yellow archangel, false lamium) can be quite invasive, though the cultivars are less aggressive. The flowers are yellow and bloom in spring to early summer. Several cultivars are available.

L. maculatum (spotted dead nettle) is the most commonly grown dead nettle. This low-growing, spreading species has green leaves with white or silvery markings and bears white, pink or mauve flowers. Many cultivars are available, including cultivars with interesting lime yellow leaves.

Also called: spotted dead nettle, lamium, yellow archangel **Features:** spring or summer flowers; decorative, often variegated foliage **Flower colour:** white, pink, yellow, mauve; plant also grown for foliage **Height:** 10–60 cm (4–24") **Spread:** indefinite **Hardiness:** zones 3–8

Eupatorium
Eupatorium

E. rugosum (above), E. maculatum (below)

Eupatoriums provide a punch of colour in a fall garden and they attract butterflies.

hese architechtural plants add volume and stature to the garden and put on a good show of late-season flowers.

Growing
Eupatoriums prefer **full sun** but tolerate partial shade. The soil should be **fertile and moist**. Wet soils are tolerated.

Tips
These plants can be used in a moist border or near a pond or other water feature. The tall types work well at the back of a border or in the centre of a bed where they can create a backdrop for lower-growing plants.

Recommended
E. coelestinum (hardy ageratum) is a bushy, upright plant that bears clusters of flossy, light blue to lavender flowers. It grows 60–90 cm (24–36") tall and spreads 45–90 cm (18–36").

E. maculatum (*E. purpureum*) is a huge plant that grows 1.5–3 m (5–10') tall and 90 cm–1.2 m (3–4') in spread. It bears clusters of purple flowers at the ends of wine purple stems. **'Gateway'** is a slightly shorter plant with much larger, rose pink flower clusters and reddish stems.

E. rugosum (*Ageratina altissima*, boneset, white snakeroot) forms a bushy, mounding clump of foliage and bears clusters of white flowers. It grows at least 90 cm–1.2 m (3–4') tall and spreads 60–90 cm (24–36"). **'Chocolate'** is a slightly smaller plant with dark purple leaves that turn dark green.

Also called: Joe-Pye weed, boneset, snakeroot **Features:** late-summer to fall flowers, foliage, habit **Flower colour:** white, purple, blue, pink, lavender **Height:** 60 cm–3 m (2–10') **Spread:** 45 cm–1.2 m (1.5–4') **Hardiness:** zones 3–8

Foamflower
Tiarella

Foamflowers form handsome groundcovers in shaded areas, with attractive leaves and billowy spikes of delicate, starry, white to light pink flowers.

Growing

Foamflowers prefer **partial, light or full shade** without afternoon sun. The soil should be **humus rich, moist** and **slightly acidic**. These plants adapt to most soils.

Divide in spring. Deadhead to encourage reblooming. If the foliage fades or rusts in summer, cut it to just above the ground. New growth will emerge.

Tips

Foamflowers combine well with fine-foliaged shade plants such as ferns and make excellent ground-covers for shaded and woodland gardens. They can be included in shaded borders and left to natural-ize in wild gardens.

Recommended

T. cordifolia (creeping foam-flower, Allegheny foamflower) is a low-growing, spreading plant that bears spikes of foamy-looking, white flowers. Many cultivars and hybrids with varied leaf shapes, colours and patterns are available. A few inter-esting and non-spreading cultivars to look for are '**Inkblot**', '**Skeleton Key**,' and '**Spring Symphony**.'

T. cordifolia (above & below)

Foamflower is in the same family and has similar foliage as Heuchera. The difference between the two lies in the flower structure, but both contrast well with fine-textured plants.

Features: spring and sometimes early-summer flowers, decorative foliage **Flower colour:** white, pink
Height: 10–30 cm (4–12") **Spread:** 30–60 cm (12–24")
Hardiness: zones 3–8

Goat's Beard
Aruncus

A. *dioicus* (above & below)

Male and female flowers are produced on separate goat's beard plants. Male flowers are said to be full and fuzzy while female flowers are more pendulous, but the difference is subtle and difficult to distinguish.

Despite its imposing size, goat's beard has a soft and delicate appearance, with divided foliage and large, plumy, cream flowers.

Growing
These plants prefer **partial to full shade**. If planted in deep shade, they bear fewer blooms. They will tolerate some full sun as long as the soil is kept evenly moist and they are protected from the afternoon sun. The soil should be **fertile, moist** and **humus rich**.

Dividing goat's beard can be a daunting task, but fortunately, these plants rarely need dividing.

Tips
These plants look very natural growing near a sunny entrance or edge of a woodland garden. They may also be used in a border, alongside a stream or pond or in a native plant garden.

Recommended
A. aethusifolius (dwarf goat's beard) forms a low-growing, compact mound and bears branched spikes of loosely held, cream flowers.

A. dioicus (giant goat's beard, common goat's beard) forms a large, bushy, shrub-like perennial with large plumes of creamy white flowers. There are several cultivars.

Features: early- to mid-summer blooms, shrub-like habit, attractive foliage and seedheads **Flower colour:** cream, white **Height:** 15 cm–1.8 m (6"–6') **Spread:** 30 cm–1.8 m (12"–6') **Hardiness:** zones 3–8

Hardy Geranium

Geranium

There is a type of geranium that suits every garden, thanks to the beauty and diversity of these hardy plants.

Growing

Hardy geraniums grow well in **full sun, partial shade** and **light shade**. These plants dislike hot weather and prefer soil of **average fertility** and **good drainage**. *G. renardii* prefers a poor, well-drained soil. Divide in spring, especially if plants flopped over the previous summer.

Tips

These long-flowering plants work well in a border; they fill the spaces between shrubs and other larger plants, and keep the weeds down. Suitable cultivars can be included in rock gardens and woodland gardens, or mass planted as groundcovers.

Recommended

G. **'Brookside'** is a clump-forming, drought-tolerant geranium with finely cut leaves and deep blue to violet blue flowers with creamy white centres.

G. macrorrhizum (bigroot geranium, scented cranesbill) forms a spreading mound of fragrant foliage and bears flowers in various shades of pink. Cultivars are available.

G. sanguineum var. *striatum* (above), *G. sanguineum* (below)

G. renardii (Renard's geranium) forms a clump of velvety, deeply veined, crinkled, sage-like foliage. A few purple-veined, white flowers appear over summer, but the foliage remains the main attraction. This is good choice for a rock garden.

G. sanguineum (bloody cranesbill) forms a dense, mounding clump and bears bright magenta flowers. Many cultivars are available, including the white-flowered **'Alba.'**

If the foliage looks tatty in late summer, prune it back to rejuvenate it.

Also called: cranesbill geranium **Features:** summer flowers; attractive, sometimes fragrant foliage **Flower colour:** white, red, pink, purple, blue **Height:** 10–90 cm (4–36") **Spread:** 30–90 cm (12–36") **Hardiness:** zones 3–8

Heuchera

Heuchera

H. americana 'Chocolate Ruffles' (above), 'Green Spice' (below)

Because of their shallow root systems, heucheras have a tendency to push themselves up out of the soil. Lift and replant them the following spring and mulch if this occurs.

With colours ranging from soft yellow-greens and oranges to midnight purples and silvery, dappled maroons, heucheras offer a great variety of foliage options for a perennial garden with partial shade.

Growing

Heucheras grow best in **light shade or partial shade**, but will tolerate full sun if well mulched. The foliage colours can bleach out in full sun, and plants grow leggy in full shade. The soil should be of **average to rich fertility, humus rich, neutral to alkaline, moist** and **well drained**. Deadhead to prolong the bloom and accentuate the stunning foliage. Every two or three years, heucheras should be dug up and the oldest, woodiest roots and stems removed. At this time, plants may be divided and replanted with their crowns at or just above soil level.

Tips

Heucheras make great contrast companions when planted in groups. Use them as edging plants, in mixed borders or grouped in woodland gardens. Combine different foliage types for an interesting display.

Recommended

There are dozens of beautiful cultivars available with almost limitless variations of foliage markings and colours, including shades of purple, burgundy, bronze and amber, some variegated or with silvery veining. Garden centres and mail-order catalogues will give you a good idea of what is available.

Also called: coral bells, alum root **Features:** spring or summer flowers, very decorative foliage **Flower colour:** red, pink, white, yellow, purple; plant also grown for foliage. **Height:** 30 cm–1.2 m (12"–4') **Spread:** 15–45 cm (6–18") **Hardiness:** zones 3–8

Hosta

Hosta

Swirls, stripes, puckers and ribs enhance the various sizes, shapes and colours of hosta foliage. New variations of this popular shade plant are introduced each year, making the selection process daunting but rewarding.

Growing

Hostas prefer **light shade or partial shade** but will grow in full shade. Morning sun is preferable to afternoon sun in partial shade situations. The soil should ideally be **fertile, moist** and **well drained**, but most soils are tolerated. Mulch to help retain moisture.

Division is not required but can be done every few years in spring as shoots emerge to propagate new plants.

Tips

Hostas make wonderful woodland plants and look very attractive when combined with ferns and other fine-textured plants. Hostas are also good plants for a mixed border, particularly when used to hide the ugly, leggy lower stems and branches of some shrubs. Hostas' dense growth and thick, shade-providing leaves help suppress weeds.

Recommended

Hostas have been subjected to a great deal of crossbreeding and hybridizing, resulting in hundreds of cultivars, including sun-tolerant and slug-resistant selections. Garden centres and mail-order catalogues will give you a good idea of what's available.

'Francee' (above)

Gardeners who think the flowers clash with the foliage remove the flowering stems when the flowers first emerge. Doing so won't harm the plants. Regardless, deadhead spent flower stalks to keep plants tidy.

Also called: plantain lily **Features:** summer and autumn flowers, decorative foliage **Flower colour:** white or purple, plants grown mainly for foliage **Height:** 10–90 cm (4–36") **Spread:** 15 cm–1.8 m (6"–6') **Hardiness:** zones 3–8

Iris

Iris

I. sibirica (above), *I. germanica* 'Stepping Out' (below)

Irises are steeped in history and lore. The name 'iris' comes from the Greek word for rainbow, and the range in flower colours of bearded irises approximates that of a rainbow.

Growing

Irises prefer **full sun** but tolerate very light or dappled shade. The soil should be of **average fertility** and **well drained**. Japanese iris and Siberian iris prefer a moist but still well-drained soil. An excessively wet soil encourages rot.

Divide in late summer, before late August. When dividing bearded iris rhizomes, cut foliage back to 15 cm (6") and replant 2.5 cm (1") deep, with the flat side of the foliage fan facing outward, away from the centre.

Deadhead irises to keep them tidy, removing only each spent flower rather than the entire stem, until all the blooms are finished. Cut back the foliage of Siberian iris in spring.

Tips

All irises are popular border plants, but Japanese iris and Siberian iris are also used alongside streams or ponds. Dwarf cultivars make attractive additions to rock gardens.

Wash your hands after handling irises; they can cause severe internal irritation if ingested. You may not want to plant them close to areas where children like to play.

Recommended

There are many iris species and hybrids available. Among the most popular are bearded irises, often hybrids of *I. germanica*. They have the widest range of flower colours but are susceptible to attack from the iris borer, which can kill a plant. Several irises are not susceptible, including Japanese iris (*I. ensata*) and Siberian iris (*I. sibirica*). Check with your local garden centre to find out what's available.

Features: spring, summer and sometimes autumn flowers; attractive foliage **Flower colour:** many shades of pink, red, purple, blue, white, brown, yellow **Height:** 10 cm–1.2 m (4"–4') **Spread:** 15 cm–1.2 m (6"–4') **Hardiness:** zones 3–8

Lady's Mantle
Alchemilla

ew other perennials look as captivating as lady's mantle when
droplets of morning dew cling like
shimmering pearls to its velvety leaves.

Growing
Lady's mantle prefers **light shade or
partial shade** and protection from the
afternoon sun. Hot locations and excessive sun will scorch the leaves. The soil
should be **fertile, humus rich, moist**
and **well drained**. Leaves can be sheared
back in summer if they begin to look
tired and heat-stressed. New leaves will
emerge. Spent flowers can be removed
to reduce self-seeding.

Tips
Lady's mantle is ideal for grouping
under trees in the dappled shade of a
woodland garden and along border and
pathway edges, where it softens the
bright colours of other plants. It also
looks attractive in containers. Compact
selections are well suited to rock gardens.

Recommended
A. alpina (alpine lady's mantle) is a low-
growing plant that reaches 7–12 cm
(3–5") in height and up to 50 cm (20")
in spread. Clusters of tiny, yellow flowers are borne in summer.

A. mollis (common lady's mantle) is the
most frequently grown species. It grows
20–45 cm (8–18") tall and spreads up to
about 60 cm (24"). This plant forms a
mound of soft, rounded foliage, and produces sprays of frothy-looking, yellowish
green flowers in early summer.

A. mollis (above & below)

*The chartreuse yellow flower sprays make
interesting substitutes for baby's breath in
fresh and dried arrangements.*

Features: summer and early-fall flowers, attractive foliage,
habit **Flower colour:** yellow, green **Height:** 7–45 cm (3–18")
Spread: 50–60 cm (20–24") **Hardiness:** zones 3–7

Lamb's Ears
Stachys

S. *byzantina* 'Big Ears' (above), S. *byzantina* (below)

Lamb's ears can ramble, but because of its shallow root system, it can easily be removed if it escapes the area in which you intended it to grow.

This plant's soft, fuzzy leaves, which are reminiscent of lamb's ears, create textural delight in the garden.

Growing
Lamb's ears grows best in **full sun**. The soil should be of **poor to average fertility** and **well drained**. The leaves can rot in humid weather if the soil is poorly drained.

Remove spent flower spikes to keep plants looking neat. Select a flowerless cultivar if you don't want to deadhead. Withered or damaged foliage can be cut back to 7–12 cm (3–5") in spring or after flowering, and fresh, new foliage will flourish.

Tips
Lamb's ears makes a great groundcover in a garden with soil that has not yet been amended. Use it to edge borders and pathways, where it will provide a soft, silvery backdrop for more vibrant colours. For a silvery accent, plant a small group of lamb's ears.

Recommended
S. byzantina (*S. olympica*) forms a mat of thick, woolly rosettes of leaves. Pinkish purple flowers are borne all summer. '**Big Ears**' ('Helen von Stein') has greenish silver leaves that are twice as big as those of the species. '**Primrose Heron**' produces primrose yellow foliage in spring that matures to chartreuse then green as the summer heats up. '**Silver Carpet**' has silvery white, fuzzy foliage. '**Big Ears**' and '**Silver Carpet**' rarely produce flowers.

Also called: woolly betony **Features:** summer flowers, decorative foliage **Flower colour:** pink, purple **Height:** 15–45 cm (6–18") **Spread:** 45–60 cm (18–24") **Hardiness:** zones 3–8

Lavender

Lavandula

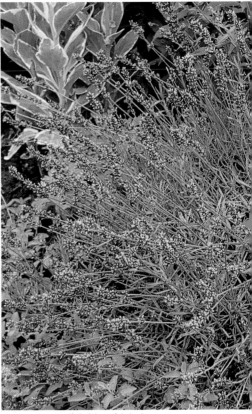

L. angustifolia (above & below)

Lavender is considered the queen of herbs. With both aromatic and ornamental qualities, it makes a valuable addition to any garden.

Growing

Lavenders grow best in **full sun**. The soil should be **average to fertile** and **alkaline,** and it *must* be **well drained**. Once established, these plants are heat and drought tolerant. Protect plants from winter cold and wind. In colder areas, lavenders should receive additional mulching and, with luck, a good layer of snow. Plants can be sheared in spring or after flowering. An older clump can easily be rejuvenated; lavender will sprout even when cut back to woody growth.

Tips

Lavenders are wonderful, aromatic edging plants. They can be planted in drifts or as specimens in small spaces, or used to form a low hedge.

Recommended

L. angustifolia (English lavender) is an aromatic, bushy subshrub that is often treated as a perennial. It grows up to about 60 cm (24") tall with an equal spread. From mid-summer to fall, it bears spikes of small flowers. Many cultivars are available, including selections with white or pink flowers, silvery grey to olive green foliage and dwarf or compact habits.

L. x *intermedia* (lavandin) is a natural hybrid between English lavender and spike lavender (*L. latifolia*). It grows 90 cm (36") tall with an equal spread. The flowers are held on long spikes. Cultivars are available.

The sensuous scent of lavender is relaxing and soothing, and it is used in aromatherapy, lavender sachets and potpourri.

Also called: English lavender, lavandin Features: mid-summer to fall flowers, fragrance, evergreen foliage, habit Flower colour: purple, pink, blue, white Height: 20–90 cm (8–36") Spread: up to 1.2 m (4') Hardiness: zones 5–8

Lungwort
Pulmonaria

P. saccharata (above & below)

Once flowering is complete, you can leave the flower stalks to wither and fade naturally. Or deadhead the plants by shearing them back lightly— this will keep the plants tidy and show off the fabulous foliage.

The wide array of lungworts display highly attractive foliage that ranges in colour from apple green to silver-spotted, and olive to dark emerald. New introductions are being released each year.

Growing

Lungworts prefer **partial to full shade**. The soil should be **fertile, humus rich, moist** and **well drained**. Rot can occur in very wet soil, but regular moisture will keep the foliage looking its best as summer heats up.

Divide in June after flowering or in September. Ensure the newly planted divisions have ample of water to help them reestablish.

Tips

Lungworts, most attractive when planted in groups, are useful and ornamental groundcovers for shady borders, woodland gardens and pond and stream edges.

Recommended

P. longifolia (long-leaved lungwort) forms a dense clump of long, narrow, white-spotted green leaves and bears clusters of blue flowers.

P. officinalis (common lungwort) forms a loose clump of evergreen foliage spotted with white. The flowers open pink and mature to blue. Cultivars are available.

P. saccharata (Bethlehem sage) forms a compact clump of large, white-spotted, evergreen leaves and purple, red or white flowers. Many cultivars are available.

Features: spring flowers; decorative, mottled foliage **Flower colour:** blue, red, pink, purple, white; plants also grown for foliage **Height:** 20–60 cm (8–24") **Spread:** 20–90 cm (8–36") **Hardiness:** zones 3–8

Meadowsweet

Filipendula

or an impressive, informal, vertical accent and showy clusters of fluffy, fragrant flowers, meadowsweet plants are second to none.

Growing

Meadowsweets prefer **partial or light shade** but tolerate full sun if the soil remains sufficiently moist. The soil should be **fertile, deep, humus rich** and **moist**, except in the case of *F. vulgaris*, which prefers dry soil. Divide in spring or autumn.

Tips

Most meadowsweets are excellent plants for bog gardens or wet sites. Grow them alongside streams or in moist meadows. Meadowsweets may also be grown at the back of a border to create a billowy accent, as long as they are well watered. Grow *F. vulgaris* if you can't provide the moisture the other species need.

Recommended

F. rubra (queen-of-the-prairie) forms a large, spreading clump and bears clusters of fragrant, pink flowers. Cultivars are available.

F. ulmaria (queen-of-the-meadow) forms a mounding clump with creamy white flowers in large clusters. Cultivars such as **'Aurea,'** with golden foliage, or **'Variegata,'** with creamy yellow and dark green variegated foliage, are available.

F. vulgaris (dropwort, meadowsweet) is a low-growing species that bears clusters of fragrant, creamy white flowers. Cultivars such as **'Plena,'** with double flowers, or **'Rosea,'** with pink flowers, are available.

F. rubra (above), *F. ulmaria* (below)

Deadhead meadowsweets if you so desire, but the faded seedheads are quite attractive when left in place, and can be used in dried flower arrangements.

Features: late-spring or summer flowers, attractive foliage **Flower colour:** white, cream, pink, red **Height:** 60 cm–2.4 m (24"–8') **Spread:** 45 cm–1.2 m (18"–4') **Hardiness:** zones 3–8

Peony

Paeonia

P. tenuifolia (above), P. lactiflora cultivars (below)

From the simple single flowers to the extravagant doubles, these voluptuous plants never fail to mesmerize. Even when the fleeting but magnificent flower display is over, the foliage remains stellar throughout the growing season.

Growing

Peonies prefer **full sun** but tolerate some shade. The planting site should be well prepared before the plants are introduced. Peonies like **fertile, humus-rich, moist, well-drained** soil to which lots of compost has been added. Mulch peonies lightly with compost in spring. Too much fertilizer, particularly nitrogen, causes floppy growth and retards blooming. Deadhead to keep plants looking tidy.

Tips

These wonderful plants look great combined in a border with other early bloomers. They may be underplanted with bulbs and other plants that will die down by mid-summer, when the peonies' emerging foliage will hide the dying foliage of spring plants. Avoid planting peonies under trees, where they will have to compete for moisture and nutrients.

In early spring, place wire peony cages around the clumps or poke twiggy branches into the soil to support the flower-bearing stems. The foliage will eventually conceal the supports.

Recommended

There are thousands of spectacular peonies available. Cultivars come in a wide range of colours, may have single, semi-double or double flowers and may or may not be fragrant. Visit your local garden centre to see the tremendous selection available.

Features: spring and early-summer flowers, attractive foliage **Flower colour:** white, cream white, yellow, pink, red, purple **Height:** 60–80 cm (24–32") **Spread:** 60–80 cm (24–32") **Hardiness:** zones 2–8

Persicaria

Persicaria

S mall, densely packed spikes of colour-ful flowers cloak these plants in late summer and fall, providing the late-season garden with much-needed colour.

Growing

Persicaria grow well in **full sun and partial shade**. Soil should be of **average fertility, moist and well drained**. Established plants are quite drought tolerant. Divide in spring or fall when clumps begin to thin out in the centre.

Tips

Persicaria make good additions to low-maintenance beds and borders. *P. affinis* is a good low-growing groundcover plant. *P. polymorpha* makes a majestic backdrop plant and can be mass planted to create a billowy deciduous screen.

Recommended

P. affinis (Himalayan knotweed) spreads to form a low mat of evergreen foliage with short spikes of flowers in shades of pale to reddish pink. Plants grow about 15–25 cm (6–10") tall and spread 30–60 cm (12–24"). Many cultivars are available, including **'Dimity'** (dwarf fleeceflower), which has light pink flowers and foliage that turns red in fall.

P. polymorpha (white fleeceflower) is a tall, clump-forming perennial that bears large clusters of creamy white flowers. Plants grow 90 cm–1.2 m (36"–4') tall and spread about 90 cm (36").

P. affinis (above), *P. bistorta* 'Superba' (below)

P. polymorpha *is becoming a favourite with landscape designers partly because of its frequent use by the world-renowned Wolfgang Oehme of Oehme & VanSweden fame.*

Also called: fleeceflower, knotweed **Features:** summer to fall flowers, low maintenance, attractive foliage, habit **Flower colour:** creamy white, pink, red **Height:** 15 cm–1.2 m (6"–4') **Spread:** 30–90 cm (12–36") **Hardiness:** zones 5–8 (could potentially survive zone 3, but this cannot be guaranteed).

Phlox

Phlox

Growing

P. paniculata and *P. maculata* prefer **full sun**, *P. subulata* prefers **full sun to partial shade** and *P. stolonifera* prefers **light shade to partial shade** but tolerates heavy shade. All like **fertile, humus-rich, moist, well-drained** soil. Divide in autumn or spring.

Tips

Low-growing species look good in rock gardens, at the front of borders or cascading over retaining walls. Taller phloxes may be used in the middle of borders and are particularly effective planted in groups.

Recommended

P. maculata (meadow phlox, wild sweet William) forms an upright clump of hairy stems with narrow leaves that are sometimes spotted with red. Pink, purple or white flowers are borne in conical clusters.

P. paniculata (garden phlox, summer phlox) is a tall, upright plant, with many cultivars in various sizes and flower colours. Look for powdery mildew-resistant cultivars.

P. subulata (above), *P. paniculata* (below)

Phlox comes in many shapes and sizes, from low creepers to tall, bushy border plants. Its fragrant flowers come in a range of colours with blooming times from early spring to mid-autumn.

P. stolonifera (creeping phlox) is a low, spreading plant that bears flowers in several shades of purple.

P. subulata (moss phlox, moss pink) is very low growing. Its flowers come in various colours and blanket the evergreen foliage. A light shearing after the plant flowers in June will encourage tidy growth and possibly a second flush of flowers.

Features: spring, summer or autumn flowers
Flower colour: white, blue, purple, orange, pink, red **Height:** 5 cm–1.2 m (2"–4') **Spread:** 30–90 cm (12–36") **Hardiness:** zones 3–8

Pinks
Dianthus

D. deltoides (above), *D. plumarius* (below)

This genus contains a variety of plants—tiny and delicate to large and robust, many with spice-scented flowers.

Growing

Pinks prefer **full sun** but tolerate some light shade. A **well-drained, neutral or alkaline** soil is required. Drainage is important—they hate to stand in water. Rocky outcroppings make up the native habitat of many species.

Tips

Pinks work well in rock gardens and rock walls, borders and walkways. They can also be used in cutting gardens and even as groundcovers. Deadhead to prolong blooming, but leave a few flowers in place to go to seed.

Recommended

D. x *allwoodii* (border pink, allwood pink) has compact mounds of evergreen foliage and flowers in a wide range of colours.

D. deltoides (maiden pink) forms a mat of foliage and red flowers, usually with a distinctive triangular pattern on the petals.

D. gratianopolitanus (cheddar pink) is long lived and forms a very dense mat of evergreen, silver grey foliage with sweet-scented flowers mostly in shades of pink.

D. plumarius (cottage pink, clove pink) flowers can be single, semi-double or fully double and come in purple, pink and white. These plants form mat-like clumps of blue-green to grey-green evergreen foliage.

Features: sometimes-fragrant spring or summer flowers, attractive foliage **Flower colour:** pink, red, white, purple **Height:** 5–45 cm (2–18") **Spread:** 15–60 cm (6–24") **Hardiness:** zones 3–8

Purple Coneflower
Echinacea

E. purpurea with *Rudbeckia* (above), E. purpurea (below)

Purple coneflower attracts birds and butterflies to the garden. Its flowerheads are popular additions to fresh or dried flower arrangements.

urple coneflower is a native wildflower renowned for its medicinal value and the visual delight it creates in the landscape. Its pinkish purple petals encircle spiky, orange centres.

Growing
Purple coneflower grows well in **full sun** or **very light shade**. It tolerates any **well-drained** soil, but prefers an **average to rich** soil. The thick taproots make this plant drought resistant, but it prefers to have regular water. Divide every four years or so in spring or autumn.

Pinch plants back or thin out the stems in early June to encourage bushy growth that is less prone to mildew. This will also encourage a later but longer blooming period. Deadhead early in the season to prolong flowering. Later you may wish to leave the flowerheads in place to self-seed and provide winter interest.

Tips
Plant purple coneflowers in meadow gardens and informal borders, either in groups or as single specimens. Purple coneflower combines well with ornamental grasses and blue- or yellow-flowered perennials and shrubs.

Recommended
E. purpurea is an upright plant covered in prickly hairs. It bears pinkish-purple flowers with conical orangey centres, and has several cultivars: **'Magnus,'** the 1998 Perennial Plant of the Year, has purple petals that stand out from the central cone; **'Razzmatazz'** has bright pink petals and a pompom-like flower form; and **'White Swan'** has white petals.

Also called: coneflower, echinacea **Features:** mid-summer to autumn flowers, persistent seedheads **Flower colour:** purple, pink, white; rusty orange centres **Height:** 60 cm–1.5 m (24"–5') **Spread:** 30–60 cm (12–24") **Hardiness:** zones 3–8

Russian Sage
Perovskia

Russian sage is a must-have plant. It offers four-season interest in the garden: soft, grey-green leaves on light grey stems in spring; fuzzy, violet blue flowers in summer and fall; and silvery white stems in fall and winter.

Growing

Russian sage prefers **full sun**. The soil should be **poor to moderately fertile** and **well drained**. Too much water and nitrogen will cause this plant's growth to flop. Russian sage cannot be divided because it is a subshrub that originates from a single stem.

In spring, when new growth appears low on the branches, cut the plant back hard to two buds, at a height of about 15–30 cm (6–12"). This will encourage bushy growth. Taller plants can be sheared or pinched back by half in May to reduce flopping and promote branching.

P. atriplicifolia (above), *P. a.* 'Filigran' (below)

Tips

Russian sage's silvery foliage and blue flowers work well with other plants in a mixed border, where it can fill spaces and provide contrast. This plant can also create a soft screen when planted in drifts.

Recommended

P. atriplicifolia is a loose, upright plant with silvery white, finely divided foliage. The small, lavender blue flowers are loosely held on silvery, branched stems. Cultivars are available, including **'Filigran,'** which has finely dissected foliage; **'Lace,'** a shorter cultivar; and **'Little Spire,'** a compact, dwarf cultivar.

Features: fragrant, mid-summer to autumn flowers; attractive habit; fragrant, grey-green foliage **Flower colour:** blue, purple
Height: 60 cm–1.5 m (24"–5') **Spread:** 60 cm–1.2 m (24"–4')
Hardiness: zones 4–8

Sedum

Sedum

S. 'Autumn Joy' (above & below)

Some 300 to 500 species of sedum are distributed throughout the northern hemisphere. Sedums are grown for their foliage, which can range in colour from steel grey-blue and green to red and burgundy. Their broccoli-like flowers bloom in mid- or late summer, then turn brown and persist through the winter.

Growing

Sedums prefer **full sun** but tolerate partial shade. The soil should be of **average fertility, very well drained** and **neutral to alkaline**. Divide in spring when needed.

Tips

Low-growing sedums make wonderful groundcovers and additions to rock gardens or rock walls. They also edge beds and borders beautifully. Taller sedums make a lovely late-season display in a bed or border.

Recommended

S. acre (gold moss stonecrop) is a low-growing, wide-spreading plant that bears small, yellow-green flowers.

S. **'Autumn Joy'** (*S.* 'Herbstfreude', autumn joy sedum) is a popular upright hybrid. The flowers open pink or red and later fade to deep bronze.

S. **'Purple Emperor'** (purple autumn stonecrop) is an upright plant with wine red to purple foliage and dusty pink flowers.

S. spectabile (*Hylotelephium spectabile*, showy stonecrop) is an upright species with pink flowers. Cultivars are available.

S. spurium (two-row stonecrop) is a popular mat-forming plant with deep pink or white flowers. Many cultivars are available and are often grown for their colourful foliage.

Also called: stonecrop Features: summer to autumn flowers; decorative, fleshy foliage Flower colour: yellow, white, red, pink, green Height: 5–60 cm (2–24") Spread: 30–60 cm (12–24") or more Hardiness: zones 3–8

Speedwell
Veronica

*M*at-forming species of speedwell wind their way around the stalks of other plants and suppress weeds, while the taller speedwells punctuate the front or middle of a garden bed with spikes of white, pink or violet flowers.

Growing
Speedwells prefer **full sun** but tolerate partial shade. The soil should be of **average fertility, moist** and **well drained**. Once established, speedwells tolerate short periods of drought. Lack of sun and excessive moisture and nitrogen may be partly to blame for the sloppy habits of some speedwells. Divide every two or three years in spring to ensure strong, vigorous growth and to reduce flopping. Strategically place short twigs in the soil to keep taller plants upright. These twigs will remain hidden by the foliage.

When the flowers begin to fade, remove the entire spike where it joins the plant to encourage rapid re-blooming.

Tips
V. prostrata works well at the front of a perennial border, as a groundcover or contained in a rock garden. Plant *V. spicata* in masses in a bed or border.

Recommended
V. prostrata (creeping speedwell) is a low-growing, spreading plant with blue or occasionally pink flowers. Many cultivars are available.

V. spicata (spike speedwell) is a low, mounding plant with stems that flop over when they get too tall. It bears spikes of blue flowers. Many cultivars with different flower colours are available.

V. spicata 'Red Fox' (above & below)

Speedwell combines well with lilies, yarrow, shrub roses and daisy-flowered perennials.

Features: summer flowers, varied habits
Flower colour: white, pink, purple, blue **Height:** 15–60 cm (6–24") **Spread:** 30–60 cm (12–24")
Hardiness: zones 3–8

Yarrow
Achillea

A. millefolium 'Paprika' (above), A. filipendulina (below)

arrows are informal, tough plants with a fantastic colour range.

These water-efficient plants make excellent groundcovers and popular additions to xeriscapes. In dried flower arrangements, the flowers retain a touch of their original colours.

Growing

Yarrows grow best in **full sun**. The soil should be of **average fertility, sandy** and **well drained**. These plants tolerate drought and poor soil. They will also tolerate heavy, wet soil and humidity, but they do not thrive in such conditions. Excessively rich soil or too much nitrogen results in weak, floppy growth. Divide every two or three years in spring.

Deadhead to prolong blooming, or shear the plant back after the first flush of blooms. Basal foliage should be left in place over the winter and tidied up in spring.

Tips

Cottage gardens, wildflower gardens and mixed borders are perfect places for these informal plants. They thrive in hot, dry locations where nothing else grows.

Recommended

A. filipendulina (fernleaf yarrow) forms a clump of ferny foliage and bears yellow flowers. It has been used to develop several hybrids and cultivars.

A. millefolium (common yarrow) forms a clump or mat of soft, finely divided foliage and bears white flowers. Many popular cultivars exist, with flowers in a wide range of interesting colours and some multi-colours.

Features: mid-summer to early autumn flowers, attractive foliage, spreading or clumping habit **Flower colour:** white, yellow, red, orange, pink, purple **Height:** 10 cm–1.2 m (4"–4') **Spread:** 30–90 cm (12–36") **Hardiness:** zones 3–8

Aralia
Aralia

A. elata (above & below)

The aralia's large leaves make this shrub look rather soft and graceful in summer, while the stout, prickly, vertical shoots offer coarse visual interest in winter.

Growing

Aralias prefer **full sun** or **light shade**. They grow best in **fertile, moist, well-drained** soil but tolerate dry, clay or rocky soil. Provide shelter from strong winds, which can dry out the foliage.

Tips

These shrubs are best suited to an informal garden. Include them in a border at the edge of a wooded area, where you won't inadvertently brush against the thorny stems.

Recommended

Both **A. elata** (Japanese angelica tree) and **A. spinosa** (Hercules' club, devil's walking stick) form large, suckering clumps and bear clusters of creamy flowers in late summer, followed by dark purple berries in fall. Foliage turns purple, orange or yellow in fall. *A. elata* is a taller plant. It has fewer thorns and doesn't sucker as much. A cultivar with variegated foliage is available. *A. spinosa* is a smaller plant and only hardy to Zone 4.

Also called: devil's walking stick, Hercules' club **Features:** foliage, flowers, fruit, stems **Habit:** deciduous small tree or large shrub **Height:** 3–9 m (10–30') **Spread:** 3–6 m (10–20') **Hardiness:** zones 3–8

Barberry

Berberis

B. thunbergii 'Atropurpurea' (above & below)

Because the devastating wheat rust fungus overwinters in some barberry species, some regions have banned all species of Berberis. *Many of these regions are now lifting the ban on* B. thunbergii *and other species that have never been proven to harbour the fungus.*

The variations available in plant size, foliage colour and fruit make barberry a real workhorse of the plant world.

Growing

Barberry develops the best fall colour when grown in **full sun**, but it tolerates partial shade. Any **well-drained** soil is suitable. This plant tolerates drought and urban conditions but suffers in poorly drained, wet soil.

Tips

Large barberry plants make great hedges with formidable prickles. Barberry can also be included in shrub and mixed borders. Small cultivars can be grown in rock gardens, raised beds and along rock walls.

Recommended

B. thunbergii (Japanese barberry) is a dense shrub with a broad, rounded habit. The bright green foliage turns shades of orange, red or purple in fall. Yellow spring flowers are followed by glossy red fruit later in summer. Many cultivars have been developed, with foliage in various shades of purple and yellow. Variegated varieties also exist.

Features: foliage, flowers, fruit **Habit:** prickly deciduous shrub **Height:** 30 cm–1.8 m (12"–6') **Spread:** 40 cm–1.8 m (18"–6') **Hardiness:** zones 4–8

Beech
Fagus

F. sylvatica 'Pendula' (above), *F. sylvatica* (below)

The aristocrats of the large shade trees, majestic beeches look attractive at any age.

Growing

Beeches grow equally well in **full sun** and **partial shade**. The soil should be of **average fertility, loamy** and **well drained**, though almost all well-drained soils are tolerated. *F. grandifolia* does not tolerate compacted soil.

American beech doesn't like having its roots disturbed and should be transplanted only when it's very young. *F. sylvatica* transplants easily and is more tolerant of varied soil and urban conditions than *F. grandifolia*.

Tips

The slow-growing beeches make excellent specimens. They are also used as shade trees and in woodland gardens. These trees need a lot of space. *F. sylvatica* can be sheared into an attractive hedge that holds its leaves until early spring.

Recommended

F. grandifolia (American beech) is a broad-canopied tree native to most of eastern North America.

F. sylvatica (European beech) is a spectacular broad tree with a number of interesting cultivars. Some are small enough to use in the home garden. Selections vary from large open trees to narrow columnar and weeping varieties. Some have purple or gold leaves or pink, white and green variegated foliage. Cutleaf selections are also available.

Beech nuts are edible when roasted.

Features: foliage, bark, habit, fall colour, fruit
Habit: large, oval, deciduous shade tree
Height: 9–25 m (30–80') **Spread:** 3–20 m (10–65') **Hardiness:** zones 4–8

Cedar
Thuja

T. occidentalis 'Yellow Ribbon' (above), T. occidentalis (below)

The rot-resistant, durable and long-lived cedar has earned quiet admiration from gardeners everywhere.

Cedar fronds are sometimes distilled for the production of cedar oils.

Growing

Cedars prefer **full sun** but tolerate light shade to partial shade. The soil should be of **average fertility, moist** and **well drained**. These plants enjoy humidity and are often found growing wild near marshy areas. Cedars perform best in locations with some shelter from wind, especially in winter, when the foliage may display winterburn.

Tips

Large selections of cedar make excellent specimen trees, and columnar cultivars work well as formal or informal hedges. Smaller cultivars can be used in foundation plantings and shrub borders.

Recommended

T. occidentalis (eastern arborvitae, eastern white cedar) is a narrow, pyramidal tree with scale-like evergreen needles. There are dozens of cultivars available, including shrubby dwarf varieties, varieties with yellow foliage and smaller, upright varieties. (Zones 2–7; cultivars may be less cold hardy)

T. plicata (western arborvitae, western redcedar) is a narrowly pyramidal evergreen tree that grows quickly, resists deer browsing and maintains good foliage colour all winter. Several cultivars are available, including dwarf varieties and a yellow and green variegated variety. (Zones 5–8)

Also called: arborvitae **Features:** foliage, bark, form **Habit:** small to large, evergreen shrub or tree **Height:** 60 cm–15 m (24"–50') **Spread:** 60 cm–6 m (24"–20') **Hardiness:** zones 2–8

Cotoneaster

Cotoneaster

C. apiculatus (above), *C. dammeri* (below)

With their diverse habits, sizes, shapes, flowers, fruit and foliage, cotoneasters are versatile enough to be used as stand-alone shrubs, groundcovers and cascading specimens.

Growing

Cotoneasters grow well in **full sun** or **partial shade**. The soil should be of **average fertility** and **well drained**. This shrub adapts to most soils.

Tips

Cotoneasters can be included in shrub or mixed borders. Low spreaders work well as groundcover and shrubby species can be used to form hedges. Larger species are grown as small specimen trees and some low-growers are grafted onto standards and grown as small, weeping trees.

Recommended

There are many cotoneaster species, cultivars and hybrids to choose from. *C. adpressus* (creeping cotoneaster) is a groundcover plant; *C. apiculatus* (cranberry cotoneaster) and *C. dammeri* (bearberry cotoneaster) are wide-spreading, low, shrubby plants. *C.* x **'Hessei'** and *C. horizontalis* (rockspray cotoneaster) are useful as low-growing groundcover; *C. salicifolius* (willowleaf cotoneaster) is an upright, shrubby plant that can be trained to form a small tree. These are just a few possibilities; your local garden centre can help you find a suitable selection for your garden.

Features: foliage, early-summer flowers, persistent fruit, variety of forms **Habit:** evergreen or deciduous groundcover, shrub or small tree **Height:** 15 cm–4.5 m (6"–15') **Spread:** 1–3.5 m (3–12') **Hardiness:** zones 4–8

Crabapple
Malus

Pure white through deep pink flowers, heights between 1.5 and 9 m (5–30') with similar spreads, tolerance of winter's extreme cold and summer's baking heat and small, yellow through candy apple red fruit that persists through winter—what more could anyone ask from a tree?

Growing
Crabapples prefer **full sun** but tolerate partial shade. The soil should be of **average to rich fertility, slightly acidic, moist** and **well drained**. However, these trees adapt to varying soil conditions.

One of the best ways to prevent the spread of crabapple pests and diseases is to clean up all the leaves and fruit that fall off the tree. Many pests overwinter in the fruit, leaves or soil at the base of the tree. Clearing away their winter shelter helps keep populations under control.

Tips
Crabapples make excellent specimen plants. Many selections are quite small, so there is one to suit almost any size of garden. Some forms are even small enough to grow in large containers. Crabapples' flexible young branches make them good choices for creating espalier specimens along a wall or fence.

Recommended
There are hundreds of crabapples available. When choosing a species, variety or cultivar, one of the most important attributes to look for is disease resistance. Many cultivars show excellent resistance to apple scab, powdery mildew and fire blight. Ask for information about new, resistant cultivars at your local nursery or garden centre. Some of the best cultivars are '**Donald Wyman,**' '**Harvest Gold,**' '**Indian Summer**' and '**White Angel.**'

Features: spring flowers, late-season and winter fruit, fall foliage, habit, bark **Habit:** rounded, mounded or spreading, small to medium deciduous tree **Height:** 1.5–9 m (5–30') **Spread:** 1.8–9 m (6–30') **Hardiness:** zones 4–8

Dogwood
Cornus

C. kousa (above), *C. kousa* var. *chinensis* (below)

There is a dogwood for almost every garden condition—wet, dry, sunny or shaded.

Growing

Dogwoods grow equally well in **full sun, light shade** and **partial shade**, with a slight preference for light shade. The soil should be of **average to high fertility, high in organic matter, neutral or slightly acidic** and **well drained**.

Tips

Shrub dogwoods can be included in a shrub or mixed border. The tree species make wonderful specimen plants and are small enough to include in most gardens. Use them along the edge of a woodland garden, in a shrub or mixed border, alongside a house or near a pond, water feature or patio.

Features: late-spring to early-summer flowers, fall foliage, stem colour, fruit, habit **Habit:** deciduous, large shrubs or small trees **Height:** 1.5–9 m (5–30') **Spread:** 1.5–9 m (5–30') **Hardiness:** zones 2–8

Recommended

C. alba (red-twig dogwood, Tartarian dogwood) and *C. sericea* (*C. stolonifera*; red-osier dogwood) are grown for their bright red, orange or yellow stems, depending on the cultivar. These provide winter interest as well as attractive fall foliage colour and fruit. (Zones 2–8)

C. alternifolia (pagoda dogwood) can be grown as a large, multi-stemmed shrub or a small, single-stemmed tree. Clusters of small white flowers appear in early summer on the attractive layered branches. (Zones 3–8)

C. kousa (Kousa dogwood) is grown for its white-bracted flowers, bright red fruit, red and purple fall foliage colour and interesting bark. (Zones 5–8)

Elder
Sambucus

S. racemosa (above & below)

Elders work well in a naturalized setting. Cultivars are available that will provide light texture in a dark area, dark foliage in a bright area or variegated yellow foliage and bright stems in brilliant sunshine.

Growing

Elders grow well in **full sun** or **partial shade**. Cultivars and varieties grown for interesting leaf colour develop the best colour in light or partial shade. The soil should be of **average fertility, moist** and **well drained**. These plants tolerate dry soil once established.

Both the flowers and the fruit can be used to make wine. All other parts of elders are toxic.

Tips

Elders can be used in a shrub or mixed border, in a natural woodland garden or next to a pond or other water feature. Cultivars displaying interesting or colourful foliage can be used as specimen plants or focal points in the garden.

Recommended

S. canadensis (American elder/elderberry), *S. nigra* (European elder/elderberry, black elder/elderberry), *S. pubens* (scarlet elder) and *S. racemosa* (European red elder/elderberry) are rounded shrubs with white or pinkish white flowers followed by red or dark purple berries. Cultivars with green, yellow, bronze or purple foliage and deeply divided, feathery foliage are available.

Also called: elderberry **Features:** mid-spring to early-summer flowers, fruit, foliage **Habit:** large, bushy, deciduous shrub **Height:** 1.5–6 m (5–20') **Spread:** 1.5–6 m (5–20') **Hardiness:** zones 3–8

Enkianthus
Enkianthus

This beautiful Japanese native is worth growing for its stunning fall colour alone.

Growing

Enkianthus grows well in **full sun, partial shade** or **light shade**. Soil should be **fertile, humus rich, moist, acidic** and **well drained**.

Tips

A perfect shrub for the understorey of a woodland garden, enkianthus also makes a good companion for rhododendrons and other acid-loving plants. It is attractive enough to be used as a specimen plant or as an alternative to a tree in a small garden.

Recommended

E. campanulatus is a large, bushy, deciduous shrub or small tree that bears small, white, red-veined, pendulous, bell-shaped flowers. The foliage turns fantastic shades of yellow, orange and red in fall. Cultivars such as **'Albiflorus,'** with white flowers, and **'Red Bells'** and **'Weston Pink Strain,'** with darker pink flowers, also make attractive additions to the garden. (Zones 4–7)

E. campanulatus (above & below)

Features: spring flowers, fall colour **Habit:** deciduous, large shrub or small tree **Height:** 3–4.5 m (10–15') **Spread:** 3–4.5 m (10–15') **Hardiness:** zones 4–7

Euonymus
Euonymus

E. alatus 'Cole's Select' (above), *E. fortunei* cultivar (below)

The versatile and adaptable euony-mus, with species ranging from deciduous shrubs to evergreen climbers, can fill a number of landscaping roles.

Growing

Euonymus species prefer **full sun** and tol-erate light or partial shade. Soil of **average to rich fertility** is preferable, but any **moist, well-drained** soil will do.

Several euonymus species form small trees or large shrubs, including E. bungeanus (winterberry euonymus), E. europaeus (spindle tree) and E. atropurpureus (eastern wahoo). These all have attractive fall colour.

Tips

E. alatus can be grown in a shrub or mixed border, as a specimen, in a natura-listic garden or as a hedge. Dwarf cultivars are often used to create informal hedges. *E. fortunei* can be grown as a hedge or as a shrub in a border. It makes an excellent substitute for the more demanding box-wood. Its trailing habit also makes it use-ful as a groundcover or climber.

Recommended

E. alatus (burning bush, winged euony-mus) is an attractive, open, mounding, deciduous shrub with vivid red fall foliage. The corky ridges, or wings, that grow on the stems and branches provide winter interest. Cultivars are available.

E. fortunei (wintercreeper euonymus) as a species is rarely grown; its attractive cultivars are more popular. These can be prostrate, climbing or mounding ever-greens, often with variegated foliage.

Features: foliage, corky stems (*E. alatus*), habit **Habit:** deciduous and evergreen shrub, small tree, groundcover or climber **Height:** 50 cm–6 m (18"–20') **Spread:** 50 cm–6 m (18"–20') **Hardiness:** zones 3–8

False Cypress
Chamaecyparis

C. pisifera 'Mops' (above), *C. lawsoniana* (below)

Conifer shoppers are blessed with a marvelous selection of false cypresses that offer colour, size, shape and growth habits not available in most other evergreens.

Growing

False cypresses prefer **full sun**. The soil should be **fertile, moist, neutral to acidic** and **well drained**. Alkaline soils are tolerated. In shaded areas, some selections may grow sparse or thin, while others are very shade tolerant.

Tips

Trees or tree forms are used as specimen plants and for hedging. The dwarf and slow-growing cultivars are used in borders and rock gardens and as bonsai. False cypress shrubs can be grown near the house or as evergreen specimens in large containers.

Recommended

There are several available species of false cypress, and many cultivars. The scaley foliage comes in a drooping or strand form, in fan-like or feathery sprays, and may be dark green, bright green or yellow. Plant forms vary too, from mounding or rounded to tall and pyramidal or narrow with pendulous branches. Several popular selections include **C. lawsoniana** (Lawson false cypress), **C. nootkatensis** 'Pendula' (Alaska cedar), **C. obtusa** (Hinoki false cypress) and **C. pisifera** (Sawara false cypress).

The oils in the foliage of false cypresses may irritate sensitive skin. These same oils make the trees very rot resistant.

Features: foliage, habit, cones **Habit:** narrow, pyramidal, evergreen tree or shrub **Height:** 50 cm–45 m (18"–150') **Spread:** 50 cm–25 m (18"–80') **Hardiness:** zones 4–8

False Spirea
Sorbaria

S. sorbifolia (above), S. s. 'Aurora' (below)

The seedheads can be removed if you find them unattractive. Even if you do leave them in place for winter interest, they should be removed in spring as the new foliage emerges.

With its feathery foliage and fleecy flowers, this shrub gives an exotic air to problem spots in the garden.

Growing

False spirea grows equally well in **full sun, partial shade** or **light shade**. The soil should be of **average fertility, moist, well drained** and **high in organic matter**. This plant tolerates hot, dry conditions.

This suckering shrub can spread almost indefinitely. Use a barrier in the soil to help prevent excessive spread. The suckering shoots can be easily removed whenever they appear in undesirable places.

Tips

Use false spirea in large shrub borders, as a barrier plant, in naturalized gardens and in lightly shaded woodland gardens. This plant can be aggressive, but its spread will be most troublesome in smaller gardens. It is ideal for steep roadway cuts and bank stabilization.

Recommended

S. sorbifolia is a large, many-stemmed, suckering shrub that bears clusters of tiny, fluffy, white or cream flowers.

Also called: Ural false spirea
Features: summer flowers, foliage
Habit: large, suckering, deciduous shrub
Height: 1.5–3 m (5–10') **Spread:** 3 m (10') or more **Hardiness:** zones 2–8

Flowering Cherry, Plum, Almond

Prunus

C herries are so beautiful and uplifting after the grey days of winter that few gardeners can resist them.

Growing

These flowering trees and shrubs prefer **full sun**. The soil should be of **average fertility, moist** and **well drained.**

Tips

Prunus species make beautiful specimen plants. Many are small enough to add to almost any garden and can be included in borders or grouped to form informal hedges or barriers. Pissard plum and purpleleaf sand cherry can be trained to form formal hedges.

Due to pest problems that afflict many of the cherries, these plants can be rather short-lived. Choose resistant species such as *P. sargentii* or *P. subhirtella*. If you plant a more suscepti-ble species, such as *P. serrulata*, enjoy it while it thrives but be prepared to replace it.

Recommended

The following are a few popular selections. **P. cerasifera 'Newport'** (Pissard plum) and **P. x cistena** (purpleleaf sand cherry) are shrubby plants grown for their purple foliage and light pink flowers. **P. sargentii** (Sargent cherry), **P. subhirtella** (Higan cherry) and **P. serrulata** (Japanese flowering cherry) are rounded or vase-shaped trees grown for their white or light pink flowers as well as their attractive bark and bright fall colour. **P. tomentosa** (Nanking cherry) bears white flowers in mid-spring and has edible, bright red fruit. The exfoliating, shiny, reddish bark is attractive in winter.

P. tomentosa (above)

Many migratory songbirds rely on the fruits of P. serotina *(black cherry) and* P. virginiana *(chokecherry) for food.*

Features: fruit, bark, fall foliage, spring to early-summer flowers **Habit:** upright, rounded, spreading or weeping, deciduous tree or shrub **Height:** 1.2–23 m (4–75') **Spread:** 1.2–15 m (4–50') **Hardiness:** zones 2–8

Fothergilla
Fothergilla

F. *major* (above & below)

Fothergilla's bottlebrush-shaped flowers have a delicate honey fragrance. These plants are generally problem free and make wonderful companions for rhododendrons and azaleas.

Flowers, fragrance, fall colour and interesting soft tan to brownish stems give fothergillas year-round appeal.

Growing
Fothergillas grow equally well in **full sun** or **partial shade**. In full sun these plants bear the most flowers and have the best fall colour. The soil should be of **average fertility, acidic, humus rich, moist** and **well drained**.

Tips
Fothergillas are attractive and useful in shrub or mixed borders, in woodland gardens and combined with evergreen groundcovers.

Recommended
F. gardenii (dwarf fothergilla) is a bushy shrub that bears fragrant, white flowers. The foliage turns yellow, orange and red in fall. **'Blue Mist'** has blue-green summer foliage and doesn't tolerate drought or poor soil conditions.

F. major (large fothergilla) is a larger, rounded shrub that bears fragrant, white flowers. The autumn colours are yellow, orange and scarlet. **'Mount Airy'** has a compact habit, lots of flowers and good, consistent fall colour.

Cultivars are available for both species.

Features: spring flowers, scent, fall foliage
Habit: dense, rounded or bushy, deciduous shrub **Height:** 60 cm–3 m (24"–10')
Spread: 60 cm–3 m (24"–10')
Hardiness: zones 4–8

Fringe Tree
Chionanthus

C. *virginicus* (above & below)

Fringe trees adapt to a wide range of growing conditions. They are cold hardy and densely covered in silky white, honey-scented flowers that shimmer in the wind in spring.

Growing

Fringe trees prefer **full sun**. They do best in soil that is **fertile, acidic, moist** and **well drained** but they will adapt to most soil conditions. In the wild they are often found growing alongside streambanks.

Tips

Fringe trees work well as specimen plants, as part of a border or beside a water feature. Plants begin flowering at a very early age.

Recommended

C. retusus (Chinese fringe tree) is a rounded, spreading shrub or small tree with deeply furrowed, peeling bark and erect, fragrant, white flower clusters on the ends of the branches. This plant needs a sheltered location to survive in zone 5. (Zones 5–8)

C. virginicus (white fringe tree) is a small, spreading tree or large shrub that bears drooping, fragrant, white flowers. (Zones 4–8)

Features: early-summer flowers, bark, habit
Habit: rounded or spreading, deciduous, large shrub or small tree **Height:** 3–7.5 m (10–25')
Spread: 3–7.5 m (10–25')
Hardiness: zones 4–8

Ginkgo

Ginkgo

G. biloba (above & below)

Ginkgo is renowned for its many medicinal properties.

Be patient with ginkgo. Its gawky, angular youth will eventually pass, leaving you with a spectacular mature specimen.

Growing

Ginkgo prefers **full sun**. The soil should be **fertile, sandy** and **well drained**, but this tree adapts to most conditions. It is also tolerant of urban conditions, compacted soil and cold weather.

Tips

Though its growth is very slow, Ginkgo eventually becomes a large tree that works best as a specimen in parks and large gardens. It is gaining popularity as a street tree. If you buy this plant, be sure to find out if it is a male or female clone. Female trees drop fruit, which becomes extremely pungent as it ripens. The stinky fruit is not something you want on your lawn, or sidewalk.

Recommended

G. biloba is variable in habit. The unique, fan-shaped leaves can turn an attractive shade of yellow in fall. Several fine cultivars are available, including **'Autumn Gold,' 'Fairmount,' 'Pendula'** and **'Princeton Sentry.'**

Also called: ginko, maidenhair tree
Features: summer and fall foliage, habit, fruit, bark **Habit:** conical in youth, variable with age; deciduous tree **Height:** 12–30 m (40–100')
Spread: 3–30 m (10–100')
Hardiness: zones 4–8

Hawthorn

Crataegus

C. laevigata 'Paul's Scarlet' (above & below)

The hawthorn is an uncommonly beautiful tree, with a generous spring show of beautiful, apple-like blossoms, persistent glossy red fruit and often good fall colour.

Growing

Hawthorns grow equally well in **full sun** and **partial shade**. They adapt to any **well-drained** soil and tolerate urban conditions.

Tips

Hawthorns can be grown as specimen plants or hedges in urban sites, lakeside gardens and exposed locations. They are popular in areas where vandalism is a problem because very few people wish to grapple with plants bearing stiff, 5 cm-long (2") thorns. As a hedge, hawthorns create an almost impenetrable barrier.

Features: late-spring or early-summer flowers, fruit, foliage, thorny branches **Habit:** rounded, deciduous tree, often with a zigzagged, layered branch pattern **Height:** 4.5–10 m (15–35') **Spread:** 3.5–10 m (12–35') **Hardiness:** zones 3–8

These trees are small enough to include in most gardens. With the long, sharp thorns, however, a hawthorn might not be a good selection if there are children about.

Recommended

C. laevigata (*C. oxycantha*, English hawthorn) is a low-branching, rounded tree with zigzag layers of thorny branches. It bears pinkish white flowers, followed by red fruit in late summer. Many cultivars are available, including **'Crimson Cloud,'** a leaf blight-resistant selection.

C. phaenopyrum (Washington hawthorn) is an oval to rounded, thorny tree that bears white flowers and persistent, shiny red fruit in fall. The glossy green foliage turns red and orange in fall.

Hemlock

Tsuga

Many people would agree that eastern hemlock is one of the most beautiful, graceful evergreen trees in the world. Its movement, grace and soft appearance make it easy to place in the landscape.

Growing

Hemlock generally grows well in any light from **full sun to full shade**. The soil should be **humus rich, moist** and **well drained**. Hemlock is drought sensitive and grows best in cool, moist conditions. It is also sensitive to air pollution and suffers salt damage, so keep it away from roadways.

Tips

Hemlock, with its delicate needles, is one of the most beautiful evergreens to use as a specimen tree. It can be pruned to keep it within bounds or shaped to form a hedge. The many dwarf forms are useful in smaller gardens.

Recommended

T. canadensis (eastern hemlock, Canadian hemlock) is a graceful, narrowly pyramidal tree. Many cultivars are available, including groundcover, pendulous and dwarf forms.

T. canadensis 'Jeddeloh' (above), *T. canadensis* (below)

The continued popularity of water gardening has put hemlock, which has a naturalizing effect within pondscapes, in high demand.

Features: foliage, habit, cones **Habit:** pyramidal or columnar, evergreen tree or shrub **Height:** 50 cm–25 m (18"–80')
Spread: 50 cm–10 m (18"–35')
Hardiness: zones 3–8

Holly
Ilex

Hollies vary greatly in shape, size and leaf form. Plant them with full consideration for their needs and they will show delightful results.

Growing

These plants prefer **full sun** but tolerate partial shade. The soil should be of **average to rich fertility, humus rich** and **moist**. Hollies perform best in acidic soil with a pH of 6.5 to 6.0 or lower. Shelter evergreen selections from winter wind to help prevent them from drying out. Apply a summer mulch to keep the roots cool and moist.

Tips

Hollies can be used in groups, woodland gardens and shrub and mixed borders. They can also be shaped into hedges. *I. verticillata* will naturalize in moist sites in the garden.

Recommended

I. glabra (inkberry) is a rounded shrub with glossy, deep green, evergreen foliage and dark purple fruit. Cultivars are available. (Zones 4–8)

I. x meserveae (meserve holly, blue holly) is a group of hybrids that originated from crosses between tender English holly (*I. aquifolium*) and hardy hollies like prostrate holly (*I. rugosa*). These dense, evergreen shrubs may be erect, mounding or spreading. (Zones 5–8)

I. x meserveae (above), *I. x m.* 'Blue Girl' (below)

I. verticillata (winterberry, winterberry holly) is a deciduous native species grown for its explosion of red fruit that persists into winter. Many cultivars and hybrids are available. (Zones 3–8)

All hollies have male and female flowers on separate plants, and both must be present for the females to set fruit. Flowering times must also coincide for pollination and fruit production to take place.

Features: glossy, sometimes spiny foliage; fruit **Habit:** erect or spreading, evergreen or deciduous shrub or tree **Height:** 1–15 m (3–50') **Spread:** 1.5–12 m (5–40') **Hardiness:** zones 3–8

Hornbeam
Carpinus

C. caroliniana (above & below)

Hornbeam leaves retain their bright, fresh green colour throughout the oppressive humidity of summer.

Attractive and slow-growing hornbeams are related to the birches and filberts. They put on an interesting display of male catkins in late summer through winter.

Growing
Hornbeams prefer **full sun** and tolerate partial or light shade. The soil should be **average to fertile** and **well drained**.

Tips
These small- to medium-sized trees can be used as specimens or shade trees in smaller gardens. *C. betulus* and its cultivars can be pruned to form large hedges. The narrow, upright cultivars are often used to create barriers and windbreaks.

Recommended
C. betulus (European hornbeam) is a pyramidal to rounded tree. The foliage turns bright yellow or orange in fall. Many cultivars are available, including narrow, upright and weeping selections. (Zones 5–8)

C. caroliniana (American hornbeam, ironwood, musclewood, bluebeech) is a small, slow-growing tree, tolerant of shady, moist and urban conditions. The foliage turns yellow to red or purple in fall. (Zones 3–8)

Features: habit, fall colour **Habit:** pyramidal, deciduous tree **Height:** 3–20 m (10–65') **Spread:** 3–15 m (10–50') **Hardiness:** zones 3–8

Horsechestnut

Aesculus

A. hippocastanum (above), *A. x carnea* (below)

Horsechestnuts range from immense, regal trees to small but impressive shrubs. All have spectacular, long-lasting flowers.

Growing

Horsechestnuts grow well in **full sun** or **partial shade**. The soil should be **fertile, moist** and **well drained**. These trees dislike excessive drought.

Tips

Horsechestnuts are used as specimen and shade trees. The roots of the horsechestnut can break up sidewalks and patios if planted too close to them. The smaller, shrubby horsechestnuts grow well near pond plantings and also make interesting specimens. Give them plenty of space as they can form large colonies.

Horsechestnuts are not edible and should not be mistaken for the edible fruit of the sweet chestnut (*Castanea*).

Recommended

A. hippocastanum (common horsechestnut) is a large, rounded tree that will branch right to the ground if grown in an open setting. The flowers, white with yellow or pink marks, are borne in long spikes. (Zones 3–7)

A. parviflora (bottlebrush buckeye) is a spreading, mound-forming, suckering shrub that has plentiful spikes of creamy white flowers. (Zones 4–8)

A. pavia (red buckeye) is a low-growing to rounded, shrubby tree with cherry red flowers and handsome foliage. It needs consistent moisture. (Zones 4–8)

Also called: buckeye **Features:** early-summer flowers, foliage, spiny fruit **Habit:** rounded or spreading, deciduous tree or shrub **Height:** 2.5–25 m (8–80') **Spread:** 2.5–20 m (8–65') **Hardiness:** zones 3–8

Hydrangea
Hydrangea

H. quercifolia (above), H. paniculata 'Grandiflora' (below)

ydrangeas have many attractive qualities, including showy, often long-lasting
flowers and glossy green leaves, some of which
turn beautiful colours in fall.

*Bigleaf hydrangea (H. macrophylla) bears
beautiful flowers in pink or blue and is hardy
in very sheltered locations in the warmest parts
of Ontario.*

Growing

Hydrangeas grow well in **full sun** or **partial shade**, and some species tolerate full shade. Shade or partial shade will reduce leaf and flower scorch in hotter gardens. The soil should be of **average to high fertility, humus rich, moist** and **well drained**. These plants perform best in cool, moist conditions.

Tips

Hydrangeas come in many forms and have many uses in the landscape. They can be included in shrub or mixed borders, used as specimens or informal barriers and planted in groups or containers.

Recommended

H. arborescens (smooth hydrangea) is a rounded shrub that flowers well even in shady conditions. This species is rarely grown in favour of cultivars such as **'Annabelle'** and **'Grandiflora,'** which bear large clusters of showy white blossoms. (Zones 4–8)

H. paniculata (panicle hydrangea) is a spreading to upright large shrub or small tree that bears white flowers from late summer to early fall. **'Grandiflora'** (Peegee hydrangea) is a commonly available cultivar. (Zones 3–8)

H. quercifolia (oakleaf hydrangea) is a mound-forming shrub with attractive, cinnamon brown, exfoliating bark. Its large leaves are lobed like an oak's, and turn bronze to bright red in fall. It has conical clusters of sterile and fertile flowers in summer. (Zones 5–8)

Features: flowers, habit, foliage, bark
Habit: deciduous; mounding or spreading shrubs or trees **Height:** 1–4.5 m (3–15')
Spread: 1–3 m (3–10') **Hardiness:** zones 4–8

Juniper
Juniperus

With all the choices available, from low, creeping plants to upright, pyramidal forms, there may be a juniper in every gardener's future.

Growing

Junipers prefer **full sun** but tolerate light shade. Ideally the soil should be of **average fertility** and **well drained**, but these plants tolerate most conditions.

Tips

With the wide variety of junipers available, there are endless uses for them in the garden. They make prickly barriers and hedges, and they can be used in borders, as specimens or in groups. The larger species form windbreaks, while the low-growing species can be used in rock gardens and as groundcover.

Recommended

Junipers vary, not just from species to species, but often within a species. *J. chinensis* (Chinese juniper) is a conical tree or spreading shrub. *J. horizontalis* (creeping juniper) is a prostrate, creeping groundcover. *J. procumbens* (Japanese garden juniper) is a wide-spreading, stiff-branched, low shrub. *J. scopulorum* (Rocky Mountain juniper) can be upright, rounded, weeping or spreading. *J. squamata* (singleseed juniper) forms a prostrate or low, spreading shrub or a small, upright tree. *J. virginiana* (eastern redcedar) is a durable tree, upright or wide spreading. Cultivars are available for all species and may differ significantly from the species.

J. procumbens 'Nana' (above), *J. horizontalis* 'Blue Prince' (below)

The juniper's prickly foliage gives some gardeners a rash. It is a good idea to wear long sleeves and gloves when handling junipers. Juniper 'berries' are poisonous if eaten in large quantities, but are often used to flavour gin.

Features: foliage, variety of colour, size and habit
Habit: conical or columnar tree, rounded or spreading shrub, prostrate groundcover; evergreen **Height:** 10 cm–25 m (4"–80') **Spread:** 50 cm–7.5 m (18"–25')
Hardiness: zones 3–8

Katsura-Tree

Cercidiphyllum

C. japonicum 'Pendula' (above), C. japonicum (below)

This tree is native to eastern Asia, and the delicate foliage blends well into Japanese-style gardens.

The Katsura-tree is a classic—it will add an air of distinction and grace to the garden. Even in youth it is poised and elegant, ready to become a bewitching, mature specimen.

Growing

Katsura-tree grows equally well in **full sun** and **partial shade**. The soil should be **fertile, humus rich, neutral to acidic, moist** and **well drained**. This tree will establish more quickly if mulched and watered regularly during dry spells for the first few years.

Tips

Katsura-tree makes a useful specimen or shade tree. The species is large and is best used in large gardens. The cultivar 'Pendula' is quite wide spreading but can be used in smaller gardens.

Recommended

C. japonicum is a slow-growing, single- or multi-stemmed tree with heart-shaped, blue-green foliage that turns yellow and orange in fall and develops a spicy scent. **'Pendula'** is one of the most elegant weeping trees available. Usually a grafted standard, its mounding, cascading branches give the entire tree the appearance of a waterfall tumbling over rocks.

Features: summer and fall foliage, habit
Habit: rounded or spreading, often multi-stemmed, deciduous tree **Height:** 3–20 m (10–65') **Spread:** 3–20 m (10–65')
Hardiness: zones 4–8

Lilac
Syringa

The hardest thing about growing lilacs is choosing from the many species and hundreds of cultivars available.

Growing
Lilacs grow best in **full sun**. The soil should be **fertile, humus rich** and **well drained**. These plants tolerate open, windy locations.

Tips
Include lilacs in a shrub or mixed border, or to create an informal hedge. *S. reticulata* can be used as a specimen tree.

Recommended
The **S. x *hyacinthiflora*** (hyacinth-flowered lilac, early-flowering lilac) group of hardy, upright hybrids become spreading as they mature. Clusters of fragrant flowers appear two weeks earlier than those of the French lilacs. The leaves turn reddish purple in fall. Many cultivars are available. (Zones 3–7)

S. meyeri (Meyer lilac) is a compact, rounded shrub that bears fragrant pink or lavender flowers. (Zones 3–7)

S. reticulata (Japanese tree lilac) is a rounded large shrub or small tree that bears white flowers. **'Ivory Silk'** has a more compact habit and produces more flowers than the species. (Zones 3–7)

S. vulgaris (French lilac, common lilac) is the plant most people picture when they think of lilacs. It is a suckering, spreading shrub with an irregular habit that bears fragrant, lilac-coloured flowers. Hundreds of cultivars with a variety of flower colours are available. (Zones 3–8)

A. *meyeri* 'Paliban' (above), S. *vulgaris* (below)

Deadheading plants as soon as flowering is finished will encourage larger flower buds to form.

Features: late-spring to mid-summer flowers, habit **Habit:** rounded or suckering, deciduous shrub or small tree **Height:** 1–9 m (3–30') **Spread:** 1–7.5 m (3–25') **Hardiness:** zones 2–8

Linden

Tilia

T. cordata (above & below)

Lindens tolerate heavy pruning and are a popular choice for large hedges in many countries.

Linden is a picturesque shade tree. Its signature pyramidal form and sweet-scented flowers capture the essence of summer.

Growing

Lindens grow best in **full sun**. The soil should be **average to fertile, moist** and **well drained**. Lindens adapt to most pH levels but prefer an alkaline soil. They tolerate pollution and urban conditions.

Tips

Lindens are useful and attractive street trees, shade trees and specimen trees. Their tolerance of pollution and moderate size make lindens ideal for city gardens.

Recommended

T. americana (American linden) is a broad, columnar tree with larger leaves than the other two species. It also bears fragrant flowers in summer. Cultivars are available.

T. cordata (littleleaf linden) is a dense, pyramidal tree that may become rounded with age. It bears small, fragrant flowers with narrow, yellow-green bracts. Cultivars are available.

T. tomentosa (silver linden) has a broad pyramidal or rounded habit that bears small, fragrant flowers and has glossy, green leaves with fuzzy, silvery undersides.

Features: habit, foliage **Habit:** dense, pyramidal to rounded deciduous tree **Height:** 6–20 m (20–65') **Spread:** 4.5–15 m (15–50') **Hardiness:** zones 3–8

Magnolia
Magnolia

Magnolias are beautiful, fragrant, versatile plants that also provide attractive winter structure.

Growing

Magnolias grow well in **full sun** or **partial shade**. The soil should be **fertile, humus rich, acidic, moist** and **well drained**. A summer mulch will help keep the roots cool and the soil moist.

Tips

Magnolias are used as specimen trees and the smaller species can be used in borders. Avoid planting magnolias where the morning sun will encourage the blooms to open too early in the season. Cold temperatures, wind and rain can damage the blossoms.

Recommended

Many species, hybrids and cultivars, in a range of sizes, flowering times and colours, are available. **M. x soulangiana** (saucer magnolia) is a rounded, spreading, deciduous shrub or tree with numerous pink-, purple- or white-flowering cultivars. **M. stellata** (star magnolia), is a compact, bushy or spreading, deciduous shrub or small tree with many-petalled, fragrant white flowers. Check with your local nursery or garden centre for other available magnolias.

M. x soulangiana (above), M. x liliiflora (below)

Magnolias can be slow to establish because they resent their roots being disturbed. Purchase smaller container-grown specimens in large containers and plant them in early spring to ensure the plant establishes as quickly as possible.

Features: flowers, fruit, foliage, habit, bark **Habit:** upright to spreading, deciduous shrub or tree **Height:** 2.5–12m (8–40') **Spread:** 1.5–10 m (5–35') **Hardiness:** zones 3–8

Maple
Acer

A. palmatum 'Sangokaku' (above), S. saccharinum (below)

There are dozens more maples to choose from, including small and large species, hybrids and cultivars. Explore the world of maples and you will surely find one that suits your garden perfectly.

Maples are attractive all year, with delicate flowers in spring, attractive foliage in summer, vibrant leaf colour in fall and interesting bark and branch structures in winter.

Growing

Generally maples do well in **full sun** or **light shade,** though this varies from species to species. The soil should be **fertile, moist, high in organic matter** and **well drained**.

Tips

Maples can be used as specimen trees, as large elements in shrub or mixed borders or as hedges. Some make useful understory plants bordering wooded areas; others can be grown in containers on patios or terraces. Most Japanese gardens have attractive smaller maples. Almost all maples can be used to create bonsai specimens.

Recommended

The larger maple species are some of the most popular choices for shade or street trees. Many are very large when fully mature, including *A.* **x** *freemanii* (freeman maple), *A.* **platanoides** (Norway maple), *A.* **pseudoplatanus** (sycamore maple) and *A.* **rubrum** (red maple). Smaller species, including *A.* **campestre** (hedge maple), *A.* **ginnala** (amur maple) and *A.* **palmatum** (Japanese maple) are useful in smaller gardens.

Features: foliage, bark, winged fruit, fall colour, form, flowers **Habit:** single- or multi-stemmed, deciduous tree or large shrub **Height:** 1.8–25 m (6–80') **Spread:** 1.8–21 m (6–70') **Hardiness:** zones 2–8

Oak
Quercus

The oak's classic shape, outstanding fall colour, deep roots and long life are some of its many assets. Plant it for its individual beauty and for posterity.

Growing

Oaks grow well in **full sun** or **partial shade**. The soil should be **fertile, moist** and **well drained**. Some species can be difficult to establish; transplant these only when they are young. Or look for adaptable species that establish quickly when transplanted.

Tips

Most oaks are large trees that work best as specimens in groves, parks and large gardens. Do not disturb the ground around the base of an oak; this tree is very sensitive to changes in grade.

Recommended

There are many oaks from which to choose. A few popular species are **Q. alba** (white oak), a rounded, spreading tree with purple-red fall colour; **Q. coccinea** (scarlet oak), noted for having the most brilliant red fall colour of all the oaks; **Q. robur** (English oak), a rounded, spreading tree with golden yellow fall colour; **'Fastigiata,'** is a popular and common upright cultivar; and **Q. rubra** (red oak), a rounded, spreading tree with fall colour ranging from yellow to red-brown. Some cultivars are available. Check with your local nursery or garden centre.

Q. palustris (above), *Q. alba* (below)

Acorns are generally not edible, but those that are edible must usually be processed first to leach out the bitter tannins.

Features: summer and fall foliage, bark, habit, acorns
Habit: large, rounded, spreading, deciduous tree
Height: 10–37 m (35–120') **Spread:** 3–30 m (10–100') **Hardiness:** zones 3–8

Pine

Pinus

P. mugo (above), P. strobus (below)

Pines offer exciting possibilities for any garden. Many exotic-looking pines are available with soft or stiff needles, needles with yellow bands and trunks with patterned or mother-of-pearl-like bark. Forms vary from open and upright to low and dense.

Growing

Pines grow best in **full sun**. These trees adapt to most **well-drained** soils. Some species do not tolerate polluted urban conditions, but others show very high tolerance, which has in some cases caused them to be overplanted.

Tips

Pines can be used as specimen trees, as hedges or to create windbreaks. Smaller cultivars can be included in shrub or mixed borders. These trees are not heavy feeders; fertilizing may encourage rapid new growth that is weak and susceptible to pest and disease problems.

Recommended

Pines come in tree form, such as *P. cembra* (Swiss stone pine) and *P. strobus* (white pine), and shrubby dwarf form, such as *P. mugo* var. *mugo* (mugo pine). Check with your local garden centre or nursery to find out what is available.

Features: foliage, bark, cones, habit **Habit:** upright, columnar or spreading, evergreen trees
Height: 60 cm–36 m (24"–120') **Spread:** 60 cm–18 m (24"–60') **Hardiness:** zones 2–8

Potentilla

Potentilla

Potentilla is a fuss-free shrub that blooms madly all summer. The cheery, yellow-flowered variety is often seen, but cultivars with flowers in shades of pink, red and tangerine have broadened the use of this reliable shrub.

Growing

Potentilla prefers **full sun** but tolerates partial or light shade. The soil should be of **poor to average fertility** and **well drained**. This plant tolerates most conditions, including sandy or clay soil and wet or dry conditions. Established plants are drought tolerant. Too much fertilizer or too rich a soil will encourage weak, floppy, disease-prone growth.

Tips

Potentilla is useful in a shrub or mixed border. The smaller cultivars can be included in rock gardens and on rock walls. On slopes that are steep or awkward to mow, potentilla can prevent soil erosion and reduce the time spent maintaining the lawn. Potentilla can even be used to form a low, informal hedge.

Recommended

Of the many cultivars of ***P. fruticosa,*** the following are a few of the most popular and interesting. **'Abbotswood'** is one of the best white-flowered cultivars; **'Pink Beauty'** bears pink, semi-double flowers; **'Tangerine'** has orange flowers; and **'Yellow Gem'** has bright yellow flowers.

P. fruticosa 'Tangerine' (above), *P. fruticosa* (below)

If your potentilla's flowers fade in bright sun or hot weather, try moving the plant to a more sheltered location. A cooler but still sunny area or a spot with some afternoon shade may be all your plant needs. Colours should revive in fall as the weather cools. Yellow-flowered plants are the least likely to be affected by heat and sun.

Also called: shrubby cinquefoil **Features:** flowers, foliage, habit **Habit:** mounding, deciduous shrub **Height:** 30 cm–1.5 m (12"–5') **Spread:** 30 cm–1.5 m (12"–5') **Hardiness:** zones 2–8

Redbud
Cercis

C. canadensis (above & below)

Redbud is an outstanding treasure of spring. Deep magenta flowers bloom with intensity before the leaves emerge. As the buds open, the flowers turn pink, covering the long, thin branches in pastel clouds.

Growing
Redbud will grow well in **full sun, partial shade** or **light shade**. The soil should be a **fertile, deep loam** that is **moist** and **well drained**. This plant has tender roots and does not like to be transplanted.

Tips
Use redbud as a specimen tree, a shrub in a mixed border or an understory tree in a woodland garden.

Recommended
C. canadensis (eastern redbud) is a spreading, multi-stemmed tree that bears red, purple or pink flowers. The young foliage is bronze, fading to green over the summer and turning vibrant yellow in fall. Many beautiful cultivars are available.

'Forest Pansy' is one of the most popular cultivars, grown for its stunning, dark purple foliage.

Features: spring flowers, fall foliage
Habit: rounded or spreading, multi-stemmed, deciduous tree or shrub **Height:** 6–9 m (20–30') **Spread:** 7.5–10 m (25–35')
Hardiness: zones 4–8

Serviceberry
Amelanchier

The *Amelanchier* species, mostly native to North America, are first-rate plants, bearing lacy, white flowers in spring followed by edible berries. In fall, the foliage colour ranges from glowing apricot to deep red.

Growing

Serviceberries grow well in **full sun** or **light shade.** They prefer **acidic soil** that is **fertile, humus rich, moist** and **well drained,** but they adapt to a variety of conditions and can be quite drought tolerant once established.

Tips

With spring flowers, edible fruit, attractive leaves that turn red in fall and often artistic branch growth, serviceberries make beautiful specimen plants or even shade trees in small gardens. The shrubbier forms can be grown along the edges of a woodland or in a border. In the wild these trees are often found growing near water sources, and look beautiful beside ponds or streams.

Recommended

Several species and hybrids are available. A few popular serviceberries are **A. arborea** (downy serviceberry, Juneberry), a small, single- or multi-stemmed tree; **A. canadensis** (shadblow serviceberry), a large, upright, suckering shrub; and **A. x grandiflora** (apple serviceberry), a small, spreading, often multi-stemmed tree. All three have white flowers, purple fruit and good fall colour.

A. canadensis (above), A. x grandiflora (below)

Serviceberry fruit can be used in place of blueberries in any recipe since it has a similar but generally sweeter flavour.

Also called: saskatoon, Juneberry **Features:** spring or early-summer flowers, edible fruit, fall colour, habit, bark **Habit:** single- or multi-stemmed, deciduous, large shrub or small tree **Height:** 1.2–9 m (4–30') **Spread:** 1.2–9 m (4–30') **Hardiness:** zones 3–8

Seven-Son Flower
Heptacodium

H. miconioides (above & below)

This smallish tree has fragrant, white September flowers followed by red sepals and fruit. Seven-son flower is a welcome addition to the landscape.

This plant is a fairly recent introduction to North American gardens and may not be available in all garden centres.

Growing
Seven-son flower prefers **full sun** but tolerates partial shade. The soil should be of **average fertility, moist** and **well drained**, though this plant is tolerant of most soil conditions, including dry and acidic soil.

Tips
This large shrub can be used in place of a shade tree on a small property. Planted near a patio or deck, it will provide light shade, and its fragrant flowers can be enjoyed in late summer. In a border it provides light shade to plants growing below it, and the dark green leaves make a good backdrop for bright perennial and annual flowers.

Seven-son flowers tolerates dry and salty soils. Plant it where salty snow may be shoveled off walkways in winter and where watering will be minimal in summer.

Recommended
H. miconioides is a large, multi-stemmed shrub or small tree with peeling, tan bark and dark green leaves tinged with purple in fall. Clusters of fragrant, creamy white flowers have persistent sepals (the outer ring of flower parts) that turn dark pink to bright red in mid- to late fall and surround small, purple-red fruit.

Features: habit, bark, fall flowers **Habit:** upright to spreading, multi-stemmed, deciduous shrub or small tree **Height:** 4.5–6 m (15–20') **Spread:** 2.5–4.5 m (8–15') **Hardiness:** zones 5–8

Smokebush
Cotinus

Bright fall colour, adaptability and flowers of differing colours, sizes and forms make smokebush and all its cultivars excellent additions to the garden.

Growing

Smokebush grows well in **full sun** or **partial shade**. It prefers soil of **average fertility** that is **moist** and **well drained**, but it adapts to all but very wet soils.

Tips

Smokebush can be used in a shrub or mixed border, as a single specimen or in groups. It is a good choice for a rocky hillside planting.

Recommended

C. coggygria is a bushy, rounded shrub with large, puffy plumes of flowers that start out green and gradually turn pinky grey. The green foliage turns red, orange and yellow in fall. Many cultivars are available, including **'Flame,'** which has exceptional fall colour, and purple-leaved selections like **'Royal Purple'** and **'Velvet Cloak.'**

C. coggygria 'Royal Purple' (above & below)

It is actually the seedheads rather than the flowers that create the plumey display we so admire in the smokebush. The contrast between the flowers and plumes is lovely.

Also called: smoketree **Features:** early-summer flowers, summer and fall foliage **Habit:** bushy, rounded, spreading, deciduous tree or shrub **Height:** 3–4.5 m (10–15') **Spread:** 3–4.5 m (10–15') **Hardiness:** zones 4–8

Snowbell

Styrax

S. japonica (above & below)

Snowbells are admired for their delicate, shapely appearance and dangling flowers that cluster along the undersides of the branches.

Growing

Snowbells grow well in **full sun, partial shade** or **light shade**. The soil should be **fertile, humus rich, neutral to acidic, moist** and **well drained**. Snowbells perform poorly in alkaline soils.

Tips

Snowbells can be used to provide light shade in shrub or mixed borders. They can also be included in woodland gardens, and they make interesting specimens near entryways or patios.

Recommended

S. japonica (Japanese snowbell) is a small, graceful, upright tree. It has arching branches from which white blossoms dangle in late spring.

S. obassia (fragrant snowbell) is a broad, columnar tree that bears white flowers in long clusters at the branch ends in early summer.

Features: late-spring to early-summer flowers, foliage, habit **Habit:** upright, rounded, spreading or columnar, deciduous tree **Height:** 6–12 m (20–40') **Spread:** 6–9 m (20–30') **Hardiness:** zones 4–8

Spirea
Spiraea

S. japonica 'Shirobana' (above)

Spireas, seen in so many gardens, remain undeniable favourites. With a wide range of forms, sizes and colours of both foliage and flowers, spireas have many possible uses in the landscape.

Growing
Spireas prefer **full sun**. To help prevent foliage burn, provide protection from very hot sun. The soil should be **fertile, acidic, moist** and **well drained**.

Tips
Spireas are used in shrub or mixed borders, in rock gardens and as informal screens and hedges.

Recommended
Many species and cultivars of spirea are available. **S. x bumalda** (bumald spirea) and **S. japonica** (Japanese spirea) are low, broad, mounded shrubs with pink flowers. They are rarely grown in favour of their many cultivars, which have similar pink or sometimes white flowers and brightly coloured foliage. **S. x vanhouttei** (Vanhoutte spirea) is a dense, bushy shrub with arching branches that bear clusters of white flowers. There are many more spireas available. Your local nursery or garden centre is very likely to have a good selection.

Features: summer flowers, habit **Habit:** round, bushy, deciduous shrub **Height:** 30 cm–3 m (12"–10') **Spread:** 30 cm–3.5 m (12"–12') **Hardiness:** zones 3–8

Spruce
Picea

P. abies 'Nidiformus' (above), *P. pungens* 'Moerheim' (below)

The spruce is one of the most commonly grown evergreens. It looks truly majestic when given enough space to allow its lower branches to sweep the ground.

Growing

Spruce trees grow best in **full sun**. The soil should be **deep, moist, well drained** and **neutral to acidic**. These trees generally don't like hot, dry or polluted conditions. Spruce of any size transplant fairly easily, though very large specimens may require the use of a tree spade.

Tips

Spruce are used as specimen trees. The dwarf and slow-growing cultivars can also be used in shrub or mixed borders. These trees look most attractive when allowed to keep their lower branches.

Recommended

Spruce are generally upright pyramidal trees, but cultivars may be low growing, wide spreading or even weeping in habit. *P. abies* (Norway spruce), *P. glauca* (white spruce), *P. omorika* (Serbian spruce), *P. orientalis* (Caucasian spruce), *P. pungens* (Colorado spruce) and their cultivars are popular and commonly available.

Features: foliage, cones, habit **Habit:** conical or columnar, evergreen tree or shrub **Height:** 60 cm–25 m (24"–80') **Spread:** 60 cm–7.5 m (24"–25') **Hardiness:** zones 2–8

Thornless Honeylocust

Gleditsia

Thornless honeylocust remains a popular tree for lawn and street plantings. The brilliant, deep yellow fall colour is wonderful to behold.

Growing

Thornless honeylocust prefers **full sun**. The soil should be **fertile** and **well drained**. This tree adapts to most soil types.

Tips

Use thornless honeylocust and its cultivars as street trees or specimen trees in larger yards. Smaller selections are more appropriate for smaller yards.

Recommended

G. triacanthos **var. *inermis*** is a spreading, rounded to flat-topped, thornless tree with inconspicuous flowers and sometimes long, pea-like pods that persist into fall. The autumn colour is a warm golden yellow. Many cultivars are available, including compact and weeping varieties, and varieties with bright yellow spring foliage.

G. triacanthos var. inermis (above & below)

This adaptable, quick-growing tree provides very light shade, making it a good choice for lawns.

Features: summer and fall foliage, habit
Habit: rounded, spreading, deciduous tree
Height: 4.5–30 m (15–100') **Spread:** 4.5–21 m (15–70') **Hardiness:** zones 4–8

Viburnum
Viburnum

V. opulus 'Nanum' (above), *V. plicatum* (below)

Good fall colour, attractive form, shade tolerance, scented flowers and attractive fruit put the viburnums in a class by themselves. Dozens of species and cultivars exist.

Growing
Viburnums grow well in **full sun, partial shade** or **light shade**. The soil should be of **average fertility, moist** and **well drained**. Viburnums tolerate both alkaline and acidic soils.

The fruit introduces much-needed colour to the landscape in late fall and winter. Some species and specific cultivars also exhibit exeptional fall and winter fruit show.

Tips
Viburnums can be used in borders and woodland gardens. Small tree forms are useful in smaller gardens. They also make interesting specimen plants.

Recommended
Many viburnum species, hybrids and cultivars are available. Popular choices include *V. carlesii* (Korean spice viburnum), a dense, bushy, rounded, deciduous shrub with white or pink, spicy-scented flowers; *V. opulus* (European cranberrybush, Guelder-rose), a rounded, spreading, deciduous shrub with lacy flower clusters; *V. plicatum* var. *tomentosum* (doublefile viburnum), with a graceful, horizontal branching pattern and lacy white flower clusters; and *V. trilobum* (American cranberrybush, highbush cranberry), a dense, rounded shrub with clusters of white flowers followed by edible red fruit.

Features: flowers (some fragrant), summer and fall foliage, fruit, habit **Habit:** bushy or spreading, evergreen, semi-evergreen or deciduous shrub **Height:** 50 cm–6 m (18"–20') **Spread:** 50 cm–4.5 m (18"–15') **Hardiness:** zones 2–8

Weigela
Weigela

Weigelas have been improved through breeding—specimens with more compact forms, longer flowering periods and greater cold tolerance are now available.

Growing

Weigelas prefer **full sun** but tolerate partial shade. The soil should be **fertile** and **well drained**. These plants will adapt to most well-drained soil conditions.

Tips

Weigelas can be used in shrub or mixed borders, in open woodland gardens and as informal barrier plantings.

Recommended

W. florida is a spreading shrub with arching branches and clusters of dark pink flowers. Many hybrids and cultivars are available: BRIANT RUBIDOR has yellow foliage; CARNAVAL bears flowers in red, pink and white; MIDNIGHT WINE is a dwarf selection; 'Victoria' and WINE AND ROSES have bronze and purple foliage, respectively.

Weigela is one of the longest-blooming shrubs; its main flush of blooms lasts as long as six weeks. It often re-blooms if sheared lightly after the first flowers fade.

W. florida 'Polka' (above),
W. f. 'Siebold Variegata' (middle)

W. florida (below)

Features: late-spring to early-summer flowers, foliage, habit **Habit:** upright or low, spreading, deciduous shrub **Height:** 30 cm–2.7 m (12"–9') **Spread:** 30 cm–3.5 m (12"–12') **Hardiness:** zones 3–8

Willow

Salix

S. integra 'Hakuro Nishiki' (above), *S. purpurea* 'Gracilis' (below)

These fast-growing, deciduous shrubs or trees can have colourful foliage or twisted stems, and they come in a range of growth habits and sizes.

Growing

Willows grow best in **full sun**. Soil should be of **average fertility, moist** and **well drained**, though some of the shrubby species are drought resistant.

Tips

Large tree willows should be reserved for large spaces and look particularly attractive near water features. Smaller willows can be planted in shrub and mixed borders or used as small specimen trees. Small and trailing forms can be included in rock gardens and along retaining walls.

Recommended

The following are just a few of the many popular willows available. **S. alba 'Tristis'** is a fast-growing, deciduous, rounded tree with delicate, flexible, weeping branches that sweep the ground. The young growth and fall leaves are bright yellow. **S. integra 'Hakuro Nishiki'** (dappled willow, Japanese dappled willow) is a spreading shrub with supple, arching branches that appear almost weeping. The young shoots are orange-pink and the leaves are dappled green, cream and pink. **S. SCARLET CURLS** (*S.* 'Sarcuzam') is an upright, shrubby tree with curled and twisted branches and leaves. The reddish, young stems become redder after a frost, creating an attractive winter display of twisted, red shoots.

Features: summer and fall foliage, stems, habit **Habit:** bushy or arching shrub, or spreading or weeping tree **Height:** 1.5–20 m (5–65') **Spread:** 1–20 m (3–65') **Hardiness:** zones 2–8

Witch-Hazel

Hamamelis

H. virginiana (above & below)

Witch-hazel is an investment in happiness. It blooms in early spring, the flowers last for weeks and their spicy fragrance awakens the senses. In fall, the handsome leaves develop overlapping bands of orange, yellow and red.

Growing

Witch-hazels grow best in a sheltered spot with **full sun** or **light shade**. The soil should be of **average fertility, neutral to acidic, moist** and **well drained**.

Tips

Witch-hazels work well individually or in groups. They can be used as specimen plants, in shrub or mixed borders or in woodland gardens. As small trees, they are ideal for gardens with limited space.

The unique flowers have long, narrow, crinkled petals that give the plant a spidery appearance when in bloom. If the weather gets too cold, the petals will roll up, protecting the flowers and extending the flowering season.

Recommended

H. x *intermedia* is a vase-shaped, spreading shrub that bears fragrant clusters of yellow, orange or red flowers. The leaves turn attractive shades of orange, red and bronze in fall. Cultivars with flowers in shades of red, yellow or orange are available, including **'Arnold Promise,' 'Diane,' 'Jelena'** and **'Primavera.'**

Features: fragrant, early-spring flowers; summer and fall foliage; habit **Habit:** spreading, deciduous shrub or small tree **Height:** 1.8–6 m (6–20') **Spread:** 1.8–6 m (6–20') **Hardiness:** zones 5–8

Yew
Taxus

T. baccata (above), T. cuspidata (below)

Sweeping hedges to commanding specimens, yews serve many purposes in the garden. They are some of the most reliable evergreens for deep shade.

Growing

Yews grow well in any light condition from **full sun to full shade**. The soil should be **fertile, moist** and **well drained**. These trees tolerate windy, dry and polluted conditions, and soils of any acidity, but they cannot tolerate excessive soil moisture. They also dislike excessive heat, and on the hotter south or southwest side of a building they may suffer needle scorch.

Tips

Yews can be used in borders or as specimens, hedges, topiary and groundcover.

Male and female flowers are borne on separate plants. Both must be present for the attractive red arils (seed cups) to form.

Recommended

T. x *media* (Anglojap yew), a cross between *T. baccata* (English yew) and *T. cuspidata* (Japanese yew), has the dark green needle colour of the English yew and the cold hardiness of the Japanese yew. It forms a rounded, upright tree or shrub, though the size and form can vary amongst the many cultivars. A few attractive selections include **'Andersonii,' 'Brownii,' 'Densiformis,' 'Hicksii'** and **'Runyan.'**

Features: foliage, habit, red seed cups
Habit: evergreen; conical or columnar tree, or bushy or spreading shrub **Height:** 60 cm–6 m (24"–20') **Spread:** 30 cm–9 m (12"–30')
Hardiness: zones 4–8

Altissimo

Climbing Floribunda Rose

*I*talian for 'in the highest,' Altissimo is an apt name for this high-climbing, high-quality, highly disease-resistant rose.

Growing

Altissimo grows best in **full sun**, in a **warm, sheltered location**. Soil should be **fertile, slightly acidic, humus rich, moist** and **well drained**. The canes must be attached to a sturdy support. Deadhead regularly until frost to prolong blooming.

Tips

Altissimo's stiff, sturdy stems form a bushy, spreading plant that can be grown as a large shrub or trained to climb a wall, trellis, porch or pergola.

Recommended

Rosa 'Altissimo' has large, matte, serrated, leathery, dark green foliage and single flowers borne in clusters for most of the growing season on both new and old growth. In a warm location it can grow to cover a wall, but in Ontario it generally grows smaller.

When cut, the long-stemmed blooms last a long time without fading. They can be used in a variety of arrangements.

Also called: Altus, Sublimely Single
Features: vigorous climber; slightly clove-scented, early-summer to fall flowers **Flower colour:** blood red
Height: 2.4–3 m (8–9') **Spread:** 1.5–2.4 m (5–8') **Hardiness:** zones 5–8

Apothecary's Rose
Species Rose

Growing
Apothecary's Rose prefers **full sun** but tolerates afternoon shade. Soil should be **average to fertile, slightly acidic, humus rich, moist** and **well drained**. The suckers it produces should be removed once flowering is complete. Leave spent flowers in place so the hips can form and provide winter interest.

Tips
Apothecary's Rose can be grown as a specimen, in a shrub border or as a hedge. It can be naturalized or used to prevent soil erosion on a bank that's too steep to mow. The flowers are very fragrant; plant this shrub near windows, doors and frequently used pathways.

Recommended
Rosa gallica officinalis is a bushy, rounded, vigorous, disease-resistant shrub with bristly stems and dark green leaves. One flush of semi-double flowers blooms each year in late spring or early summer. *Rosa gallica versicolor* (Rosamund's rose) has white or light pink flowers with darker pink splashes and stripes. It is a naturally occurring sport of the species.

As its common name indicates, this rose, which has been cultivated since the 13th century, was and still is used for medicinal purposes.

Also called: Red Damask, Red Rose of Lancaster
Features: rounded habit; fresh and intensely fragrant, early-summer flowers; dark red hips
Flower colour: crimson purple, pinkish red, light pink, white **Height:** 75 cm–1.2 m (30"–4')
Spread: 75 cm–1.2 m (30"–4')
Hardiness: zones 3–8

Belle Amour

Old Garden Rose

*C*lassified as an ancient damask rose, this low-maintenance and disease-resistant plant is extremely easy to grow.

Growing
Belle Amour grows best in **full sun**. The soil should be **average to fertile, humus rich, slightly acidic, moist** and **well drained**, but it tolerates most soil conditions once it's established.

Tips
Old garden roses like Belle Amour look best in English country-style gardens, but they can be used in borders and as specimens.

Recommended
Rosa '**Belle Amour**' is an upright shrub with grey-green foliage. It bears fully double, camellia-like blooms in a single flush in late spring or early summer. The bright red hips persist into winter, but they will not form if the plant is deadheaded.

Old garden roses, the ancestors of many roses found today, were discovered or hybridized before 1867. They are admired for their delicate beauty, old-fashioned appearances and fantastic fragrances.

Features: upright habit; spicy, myrrh-scented, early-summer flowers; red hips
Flower colour: light to medium pink
Height: 1.5–1.8 m (5–6') **Spread:** 90 cm–1.2 m (3–4') **Hardiness:** zones 3–8

Cupcake
Miniature Rose

Cupcake can be brought indoors for the winter and admired as a houseplant until spring. It will do best in a cool, well-ventilated room.

Cupcake has strong, healthy growth and it blooms throughout the season. It is a disease-resistant, thornless miniature rose that requires very little maintenance.

Growing
Cupcake grows best in **full sun**. Soil should be **fertile, humus rich, slightly acidic, moist** and **well drained**. Deadhead to keep plants neat and encourage continuous blooming.

Tips
Miniature roses like Cupcake are sometimes used as annual bedding plants. As annual or perennial shrubs they can be included in window boxes, planters and mixed containers. In a bed or border they can be grouped together or planted individually to accentuate specific areas. Try planting them en masse as groundcover or to create a low hedge.

Recommended
Rosa '**Cupcake**' is a compact, bushy shrub with glossy, green foliage that resembles a miniature version of a high-centered, large-flowered modern rose. It produces small clusters of double flowers all summer.

Features: bushy habit; slightly fragrant, early-summer to fall flowers
Flower colour: light to medium pink
Height: 30–45 cm (12–18")
Spread: 30–35 cm (12–14")
Hardiness: zones 5–8

Dainty Bess

Hybrid Tea Rose

*W*hen Dainty Bess is in flower, it is truly one of the most beautiful roses imaginable.

Growing

Dainty Bess grows best in **full sun** in a **warm, sheltered location**. Soil should be **fertile, humus rich, slightly acidic, moist** and **well drained**. Deadhead to keep plants tidy and encourage continuous blooming. Protection will be required to successfully overwinter this rose.

Tips

Dainty Bess' unique flowers make it a wonderful specimen plant for a small garden. It can also be planted in small groups in a mixed or shrub border. If you plant it close to the house for shelter, be sure to water it regularly; sheltered locations often lack moisture.

Recommended

Rosa **'Dainty Bess,'** sometimes called the Artistic Rose, has leathery, dark green leaves and clusters of single flowers that close at night all summer. A climbing form is also available.

Hybrid tea roses generally have large, double, long-lasting flowers in a wide range of colours. Dainty Bess' single flowers are quite unusual for a hybrid tea.

Also called: Artistic Rose **Features:** bushy, branching habit; fragrant, ruffled, early-summer to fall flowers **Flower colour:** pale pink with burgundy stamens **Height:** 90 cm–1.2 m (3–4') **Spread:** 60–90 cm (24–36") **Hardiness:** zones 5–8

Flower Carpet

Groundcover Rose

These roses bloom in such abundance that the flowers form a carpet, hence the name Flower Carpet. Deadheading will keep plants tidy and blooming enthusiastically.

Since their release in 1991, the Flower Carpet roses have proven themselves to be low-maintenance, blackspot-resistant, long-blooming performers in the landscape.

Growing

Flower Carpet roses grow best in **full sun**. The soil should be **average to fertile, humus rich, slightly acidic, moist** and **well drained,** but this hardy rose is fairly adaptable.

Tips

Though not true groundcovers, these small shrub roses have dense and spreading habits useful for filling in large areas. They can also be used as low hedges or in mixed border. Their sometimes long, rangy canes may require some pruning to reduce their spread. Flower Carpet roses even grow well near roads, sidewalks and driveways where salt is applied in winter.

Recommended

The *Rosa* **'Flower Carpet'** roses are bushy, low-growing, spreading plants with shiny, bright green, leathery foliage. They produce single or semi-double flowers in white, yellow, pink, coral, red, or apple-blossom, with prominent yellow stamens. These flowers last from early summer through fall to the first heavy frost.

Features: mounding, spreading habit; summer through fall flowers **Flower colour:** deep hot pink, white, coral, red, apple-blossom **Height:** 75–90 cm (30–36") **Spread:** 90–1.2 m (3–4') **Hardiness:** zones 4–8

Golden Celebration

English (Austin) Rose

David Austin roses are famous for their scents and Golden Celebration is no exception. Its fruity aroma is strong enough to catch the attention of any passerby.

Growing

Golden Celebration, like all Austin roses, grows best in **full sun** in a **warm, sheltered location**. Soil should be **fertile, humus rich, slightly acidic, moist** and **well drained**. Deadhead to keep plants tidy and encourage continuous blooming. Protection may be required to overwinter this and other Austin roses successfully.

Tips

Austin roses such as Golden Celebration have many uses. They are often grouped in borders or used as stunning specimens. With training, Golden Celebration can also be used as a climber. Plant it near a window, door or pathway where its fragrance can be enjoyed.

Recommended

Rosa '**Golden Celebration**' forms a rounded shrub with dark green, glossy foliage and flexible canes that sway or bend under the weight of the double flowers. Other Austin roses are available in shades of pink ('**Eglantyne**'), orange ('**Pat Austin**'), apricot ('**Evelyn**'), yellow ('**Graham Thomas**') and white ('**Rose Marie**').

Golden Celebration is considered one of the largest-flowered and most stunning Austin roses ever developed.

Features: attractive, rounded habit; fruity-scented, early-summer to fall flowers
Flower colour: golden yellow
Height: 1.2–1.5 m (4–5') **Spread:** 1.2–1.5 m (4–5') **Hardiness:** zones 5–8

Hansa

Rugosa Shrub Rose

ansa, first introduced in 1905, is one of the most durable, long-lived and versatile roses.

Growing

Hansa grows best in **full sun**. Soil should preferably be **average to fertile, humus rich, slightly acidic, moist** and **well drained,** but this durable rose adapts to most soils, from sandy to silty clay. Remove a few of the oldest canes every few years to keep plants blooming vigorously.

Tips

Rugosa roses like Hansa make good additions to mixed borders and beds, and can also be used as hedges or as specimens. These salt-tolerant roses are often planted along paths and roadsides, or on steep banks to prevent soil erosion. Their prickly branches deter people from walking across flowerbeds and compacting the soil.

Recommended

Rosa **'Hansa'** is a bushy shrub with arching canes and leathery, deeply veined, bright green leaves. The fragrant double flowers are produced all summer, and bright orange hips persist into winter. Other rugosa roses include **'Blanc Double de Coubert,'** which produces white, double flowers all summer.

Features: dense, arching habit; clove-scented, early-summer to fall flowers; orange-red hips; colourful fall foliage **Flower colour:** mauve purple or mauve red **Height:** 1.2–1.5 m (4–5') **Spread:** 1.5–1.8 m (5–6') **Hardiness:** zones 3–8

Hope For Humanity

Parkland Shrub Rose

Introduced in 1995, Hope for Humanity was named in honour of the 100th anniversary of the Canadian Red Cross Society.

Growing

Hope for Humanity grows best in **full sun**. Soil should be **fertile, humus rich, slightly acidic, moist** and **well drained**. Hope for Humanity's foliage is resistant to mildew and rust, but somewhat susceptible to blackspot.

Tips

This small, attractive shrub rose makes a good addition to a mixed bed or border, and it looks attractive when planted in groups of three or more. Its small stature also makes it a popular choice for containers and large planters, although some winter protection may be needed for plants not grown directly in the ground.

Recommended

Rosa **'Hope for Humanity'** is a compact, low-growing shrub with glossy, dark green foliage and double flowers that bloom continuously for months. The Parkland rose series boasts a wide range of flower colours, some of which are uncommon in hardy shrub roses. Other roses in the series include **'Morden Blush,' 'Morden Fireglow,' 'Morden Sunrise'** and **'Prairie Joy.'**

The Parkland roses, a series of hardy roses and mostly compact shrubs, were developed in Brandon, Manitoba to withstand prairie winters. They perform equally well in warmer regions of Ontario.

Features: compact habit; lightly scented, midsummer to fall flowers **Flower colour:** intense blood red with a small white spot at the petal base and a white or yellow spot on the outer margin of each petal **Height:** 60 cm (24") **Spread:** 60 cm (24") **Hardiness:** zones 3–8

Iceberg
Floribunda Rose

Over 40 years have passed since this exceptional rose was first introduced into commerce and its continued popularity proves it can stand the test of time.

Growing

Iceberg grows best in **full sun**. Soil should be **fertile, humus rich, slightly acidic, moist** and **well drained**. Winter protection is required. Deadhead to prolong blooming.

Iceberg's profuse blooms almost obscure its foliage. Remove the blooms as they fade to keep the plant blooming until the first hard fall frost.

Tips

Iceberg is a popular addition to mixed borders and beds, and it also works well as a specimen. Plant it in a well-used area or near a window where its flower fragrance can best be enjoyed. This rose can also be included in large planters or patio containers.

Recommended

Rosa 'Iceberg' is a vigorous bush with a rounded, bushy habit and light green foliage. It produces clusters of semi-double flowers in several flushes from early summer to fall. A climbing variation of this rose is reputed to be the best climbing white rose ever developed.

Also called: Fée des Neiges **Features:** bushy habit; strong, sweet fragrance; early-summer to fall flowers **Flower colour:** white, sometimes flushed with pink during cool or wet weather **Height:** 90 cm–1.2 m (3–4') **Spread:** 90 cm–1.2 m (3–4') **Hardiness:** zones 5–8

John Cabot

Explorer Shrub Rose

John Cabot was introduced in 1978 as the first climbing Explorer rose and is still considered one of the best in the series.

Growing

John Cabot grows best in **full sun** but tolerates some afternoon shade. The soil should be **average to fertile, humus rich, slightly acidic, moist** and **well drained**. Deadhead to keep plants tidy. Trim back any tips that show winter damage in spring.

Tips

John Cabot is best trained as a climber but performs equally well when pruned to form a shrub. Train the branches to climb on a decorative support such as a pergola, archway, fence or obelisk. This rose also looks attractive in mixed beds or borders, especially when it has room to display its open, cascading habit.

Recommended

Rosa 'John Cabot' has bright green foliage and produces profuse, semi-double flowers all summer. Roses in the Explorer series, all named after explorers of Canada such as '**Champlain**,' '**Henry Hudson**' and '**Martin Frobisher**,' come in a variety of flower colours and sizes. All have been bred for cold hardiness.

Features: trailing habit; sweet-scented, mid-summer to fall flowers **Flower colour:** bright pink, magenta **Height:** 2.4–3 m (8–10') **Spread:** 1.5–1.8 m (5–6') **Hardiness:** zones 3–8

Queen Elizabeth
Grandiflora Rose

The grandiflora classification was originally created to accommodate this rose. Queen Elizabeth is one of the most widely grown and best-loved roses.

Growing
Queen Elizabeth grows best in **full sun.** Soil should preferably be **average to fertile, humus rich, slightly acidic, moist** and **well drained,** but this durable rose adapts to most soils and tolerates high

Queen Elizabeth has won many honours and was named World's Favorite Rose in 1979.

heat and humidity. Prune plants back to 5–7 canes, and to 5–7 buds each spring.

Tips
Queen Elizabeth is a trouble-free rose that makes a good addition to mixed borders and beds. It can also be used as a specimen or to form a hedge. Or try growing it in a large planter. Its flowers are borne on sturdy stems that make them useful for floral arrangements.

Recommended
Rosa '**Queen Elizabeth'** is a bushy plant with glossy, dark green foliage and dark stems. The pink, cup-shaped, double flowers may be borne singly or in clusters of several flowers.

Features: glossy, dark green, disease-resistant foliage; lightly scented, summer to fall flowers
Flower colour: soft, pearly pink **Height:** 1.2–1.8 m (4–6') **Spread:** 75–90 cm (30–36")
Hardiness: zones 5–8

Rosa glauca
Species Rose

This species rose is a gardener's dream; it's hardy and disease resistant with striking foliage in summer and colourful hips in winter.

Growing

Rosa glauca grows best and develops contrasting foliage colour in **full sun**, but it tolerates some shade. Soil should be **average to fertile, humus rich, slightly acidic, moist** and **well drained,** but this rose adapts to most soils, from sandy soil to silty clay.

Remove a few of the oldest canes to the ground every few years to encourage younger, more colourful stems to grow in. Removing spent flowers won't prolong the blooming period, and the more flowers you leave the more hips will form.

Also called: Red-leaved Rose **Features:** dense, arching habit; purple- or red-tinged foliage; late-spring flowers; persistent dark red hips **Flower colour:** mauve pink with white centres **Height:** 1.8–3 m (6–10') **Spread:** 1.5–1.8 m (5–6') **Hardiness:** zones 2–8

Tips

With its unusual foliage colour, *Rosa glauca* makes a good addition to mixed borders and beds, and it can also be used as a hedge or a specimen.

Recommended

Rosa glauca (*R. rubrifolia*) is a bushy shrub with arching, purple-tinged canes and delicate, purple-tinged, blue-green leaves. The single, star-like flowers bloom in clusters in late spring. The dark red hips persist until spring.

Rosa glauca is extremely popular with rosarians and novice gardeners alike because of its hardiness, disease resistance, dainty blooms and foliage colour. It received the Royal Horticultural Society Award of Garden Merit, proof of its dependable performance.

Rosemary Harkness

Hybrid Tea Rose

These beautiful, uniquely coloured flowers are welcome additions to the garden or any flower arrangement, and are sure to become a conversation piece.

Rosemary Harkness is often the first hybrid tea rose to bloom in late spring or early summer.

Growing

Rosemary Harkness grows best in **full sun** in a **warm, sheltered location**. Soil should be **fertile, humus rich, slightly acidic, moist** and **well drained**. This rose likes a very fertile soil; amending the soil with **additional organic matter** will improve its nutrient content, texture, water retention and drainage. Winter protection is required to overwinter this rose successfully.

Tips

Rosemary Harkness has stunning flowers and works best as a specimen plant, but it can be used in a mixed border with shallow-rooted plants that will not compete excessively for water and nutrients. Plant it where you can enjoy its fragrant flowers.

Recommended

Rosa '**Rosemary Harkness**' is a vigorous, shrubby rose with glossy, dark green leaves. It produces large, fully double flowers from early summer until frost.

There are thousands more spectacular hybrid tea roses to choose from, in every colour except blue.

Features: spreading habit; sweet, fruity-scented, late-spring to fall flowers **Flower colour:** apricot yellow with salmon pink edges **Height:** 75 cm (30") **Spread:** 75 cm (30") **Hardiness:** zones 5–8

Black-Eyed Susan Vine
Thunbergia

Black-eyed Susan vine is a useful flowering vine with simple, five-petalled flowers that give it a cheerful appearance.

Growing

Black-eyed Susan vines do well in **full sun**, **partial shade** or **light shade**. Grow them in **fertile, moist, well-drained** soil that is high in **organic matter**.

Tips

Black-eyed Susan vines can be trained to twine up and around fences, walls, trees and shrubs. They also look attractive in mixed containers, window boxes and hanging baskets, or trailing down from the top of a rock garden or rock wall.

Recommended

T. alata is a vigorous, twining climber. It bears yellow flowers, often with dark centres, in summer and fall. Cultivars with large flowers in yellow, orange or white are available.

T. grandiflora (skyflower vine, blue trumpet vine) is less commonly available than *T. alata*. It tends to bloom late, in early to mid-fall. This twining climber bears stunning, pale violet blue flowers. **'Alba'** has white flowers.

T. alata (above & below)

Black-eyed Susan vine blooms are actually trumpet shaped; their dark centres or 'eyes' form a tube.

Features: twining habit **Flower colour:** yellow, orange, violet blue, creamy white; dark-centred
Height: 1.5 m (5') **Spread:** 1.5 m (5')
Hardiness: tender perennial treated as an annual

Clematis

Clematis

C. x *jackmanii* (above), C. 'Gravetye Beauty' (below)

Prune your clematis depending on when it blooms: prune spring bloomers after flowering and summer bloomers in early spring.

For a horticultural treat, try interplanting clematis with climbing roses. Whether they bloom at the same time or one after the other, the show is sure to be impressive.

Growing

Clematis plants prefer **full sun** but tolerate partial shade. The soil should be **fertile, humus rich, moist** and **well drained**. These vines enjoy warm, sunny weather, but the roots prefer to stay cool. A thick layer of mulch or a planting of low, shade-providing perennials will protect the tender roots. Clematis are quite cold hardy but fare best when protected from winter wind. A vining clematis' rootball should be planted about 5 cm (2") beneath the soil surface.

Tips

Clematis vines can climb up structures such as trellises, railings, fences and arbours. They can also grow over shrubs and up trees. Some types can be used as groundcovers.

Recommended

There are many species, hybrids and cultivars of clematis. The flower forms, blooming times and sizes of the plants can vary. Check with your local garden centre to see what is available.

Features: twining habit, decorative seedheads, early- to late-summer flowers **Flower colour:** blue, purple, pink, yellow, red or white; solid, mottled or striped **Height:** 3–5 m (10–17') or more **Spread:** 1.5 m (5') or more **Hardiness:** zones 3–8

Climbing Hydrangea

Hydrangea

H. anomala subsp. *petiolaris* (above & below)

A mature climbing hydrangea can cover an entire wall. With its dark, glossy leaves and delicate, lacy flowers, it is quite possibly one of the most stunning climbing plants available.

Growing

Hydrangeas prefer **partial shade** or **light shade** but tolerate both full sun and full shade. The soil should be of **average to high fertility, humus rich, moist** and **well drained**. These plants perform best in cool, moist conditions, so be sure to mulch their roots.

Tips

Climbing hydrangea climbs up trees, walls, fences, pergolas and arbours. It clings to walls with aerial roots, and needs no support other than a somewhat textured surface. It also grows over rocks and can be used as a groundcover or trained to form a small tree or shrub.

Recommended

H. anomala subsp. *petiolaris* (*H. petiolaris*) is a clinging deciduous vine with dark, glossy green leaves that sometimes turn an attractive yellow in fall. For more than a month in mid-summer, the vine is covered with white, lacy-looking flowers, and the entire plant appears to be veiled in a lacy mist in June.

Features: flowers, clinging habit, exfoliating bark **Flower colour:** white **Height:** 15–25 m (50–80') **Spread:** 15–25 m (50–80') **Hardiness:** zones 4–8

Cup-and-Saucer Vine
Cobaea

C. scandens (above & below)

Cup-and-saucer vine is a vigorous climber native to Mexico that produces frilly, purple flowers from spring until frost.

Growing

Cup-and-saucer vine prefers **full sun**. The soil should be **well drained** and of **average fertility**. This plant is fond of hot weather and will grow best in a sheltered site with southern exposure. Set the seeds on edge when planting them, and barely cover them with soil. They will take over two weeks to germinate.

Tips

Grow this vine up a trellis, over an arbour or along a chain-link fence. Cup-and-saucer vine uses grabbing hooks to climb and therefore needs a sturdy support, such as a trellis or coarse-textured wall, to grab. It can be trained to fill almost any space. In a hanging basket, the vines will climb the hanger and spill over the edges.

Recommended

C. scandens is a vigorous climbing vine with flowers that are creamy green when they open and mature to deep purple. For white flowers, try **var. *alba***.

Also called: cathedral bells **Features:** clinging habit, long blooming period **Flower colour:** purple, white **Height:** 4.5–7.5 m (15–25') **Spread:** 4.5–7.5 m (15–25') **Hardiness:** tender perennial, treated as an annual

English Ivy
Hedera

H. helix (above & below)

One of the loveliest things about English ivy is the variation in green and blue tones it adds to the garden.

Growing

English ivy prefers **light shade** or **partial shade** but will adapt to any light conditions, from full shade to full sun. The foliage can become damaged or dried out in winter if the plant is grown in a sunny, exposed site. The soil should be of **average to rich fertility, moist** and **well drained**. The richer the soil, the better this vine will grow.

Tips

English ivy is grown as a trailing groundcover or as a climbing vine. It clings tenaciously to exterior walls, tree trunks, stumps and many other rough-textured surfaces. Ivy rootlets can damage walls and fences, but cold Ontario winters prevent the rampant growth that makes this plant troublesome and invasive in warmer climates.

Recommended

H. helix is a vigorous plant with dark, glossy, triangular, evergreen leaves that may be tinged with bronze or purple in winter, adding another season of interest to your garden. Many cultivars have been developed, some for increased cold hardiness. Others have interesting, often variegated foliage, but are not exceptionally hardy. Check with your local garden centre to see what is available.

Also called: common ivy **Features:** foliage, climbing or trailing habit **Height:** indefinite **Spread:** indefinite **Hardiness:** zones 5–8

Hardy Kiwi
Actinidia

A. arguta 'Ananasnaya' (above), *A. arguta* (below)

Hardy kiwi is handsome in its simplicity, and its lush green leaves, vigour and adaptability make it very useful, especially on difficult sites.

Growing
Hardy kiwi vines grow best in **full sun**, but they tolerate light shade with reduced fruit production and less foliage variegation. The soil should be **fertile** and **well drained**. These plants require shelter from strong winds. Protect them from cats until they are established; the hardy kiwi's sap sometimes produces a catnip-like effect.

Tips
These vines need a sturdy structure to twine around. Pergolas, arbours and sufficiently large and sturdy fences provide good support. Given a trellis against a wall, a tree or some other upright structure, hardy kiwis will twine upward all summer. They can also be grown in containers.

Hardy kiwi vines can grow uncontrollably. Don't be afraid to prune them back if they are getting out of hand. Fruit production can be increased by pruning kiwi vines in the same way as grape vines.

Recommended
There are two hardy kiwi vines commonly grown in Canadian gardens. *A. arguta* (hardy kiwi, bower actinidia) has dark green, heart-shaped leaves, white flowers and smooth-skinned, greenish yellow, edible fruit. *A. kolomikta* (variegated kiwi vine, kolomikta actinidia) has green leaves strongly variegated with pink and white, white flowers and smooth-skinned, greenish yellow, edible fruit.

Features: early-summer flowers, edible fruit, twining habit **Flower colour:** white **Height:** 4.5–9 m (15–30') to indefinite **Spread:** 4.5–9 m (15–30') to indefinite **Hardiness:** zones 3–8

Honeysuckle

Lonicera

Honeysuckles can be rampant, twining vines, but with careful consideration and placement, they won't overrun your garden. The fragrance of the flowers makes any effort worthwhile, and the honeysuckle berries will attract birds.

Growing

Honeysuckles grow well in **full sun** or **partial shade**. The soil should be **average to fertile, humus rich, moist** and **well drained**.

Tips

Honeysuckle can be trained to grow up a trellis, fence, arbour or other structure. In a large container near a porch it will ramble over the edges and up the railings with reckless abandon.

Recommended

There are dozens of honeysuckle species, hybrids and cultivars. Check with your local garden centre to see what is available. The following are popular choices.

L. caprifolium (Italian honeysuckle, Italian woodbine) bears fragrant, creamy white or yellow flowers in late spring and early summer.

L. japonica **'Aureo-reticulata'** has dark green leaves variegated with a lacy yellow overlay.

L. sempervirens (trumpet honeysuckle, coral honeysuckle) bears orange or red flowers in late spring and early summer. Many cultivars and hybrids are available with flowers in yellow, red or scarlet,

L. x *brownii* 'Dropmore Scarlet' (above & below)

including *L.* x *brownii* **'Dropmore Scarlet,'** one of the hardiest climbing honeysuckles (cold hardy to zone 4). It bears bright red flowers for most of the summer.

Features: late-spring and early-summer flowers, twining habit, fruit **Flower colour:** creamy white, yellow, orange, red, scarlet **Height:** 1.8–6 m (6–20') **Spread:** 1.8–6 m (6–20') **Hardiness:** zones 5–8

Hops
Humulus

H. lupulus (above & below)

Hops are herbaceous perennials; each year the plant sends up shoots from ground level. Cut them back completely, just above the ground, in early spring to make way for the new growth.

*I*f you sit nearby for an afternoon, you might be able to see your hops grow.

Growing
Hops grow best in **full sun**. The soil should be **average to fertile, humus rich, moist** and **well drained**, although established plants will adapt to most conditions as long as they are well watered for the first few years.

Tips
Hops will quickly twine around a sturdy support to create a screen or shade a patio or deck. Provide a pergola, arbour, porch rail or even a telephone pole for support. Most trellises are too delicate for this vigorous grower.

Recommended
H. lupulus is a fast-growing, twining vine with rough-textured, bright green leaves and stems. The fragrant, cone-like flowers—used to flavour beer—are produced only on the female plants. **'Aureus,'** a shade-tolerant cultivar with golden yellow foliage, will also withstand full sun.

Features: twining habit; dense growth; cone-like, late-summer flowers **Height:** 3–6 m (10–20') **Spread:** 3–6 m (10–20') **Hardiness:** zones 3–8

Japanese Hydrangea Vine

Schizophragma

This woody perennial vine resembles a climbing hydrangea in appearance, but it has a few interesting cultivars that add variety.

Growing

Japanese hydrangea vine grows well in **full sun** or **partial shade**. The soil should be **average to fertile, humus rich, moist** and **well drained**.

This vine will have trouble clinging to a smooth-surfaced wall. Attach a few supports to the wall and tie the vines to these supports. The dense growth will eventually hide the supports.

Tips

Japanese hydrangea vine will cling to any rough surface and looks attractive climbing a wall, fence, tree, pergola or arbour. It can also be used as a ground-cover on a bank or grown up or over a rock wall.

Recommended

S. hydrangeoides is an attractive deciduous climbing vine, similar in appearance to climbing hydrangea. It bears lacy clusters of white flowers for several weeks in mid-summer. **'Moonlight'** has silvery blue foliage. **'Roseum'** bears clusters of pink flowers.

S. hydrangeoides (above & below)

This elegant vine can add a touch of glamour to any garden.

Features: clinging habit, dark green or silvery foliage **Flower colour:** white, pink **Height:** up to 12 m (40') **Spread:** up to 12 m (40') **Hardiness:** zones 5–8

Sweet Pea
Lathyrus

L. odoratus (above & below)

Sweet peas are among the most enchanting annuals. Their fragrance is intoxicating and the flowers bloom in double tones and shimmering shades like no other annual in the garden.

Growing
Sweet peas prefer **full sun** but tolerate light shade. The soil should be **fertile,** high in **organic matter, moist** and **well drained**. The plants tolerate light frost.

Soak seeds in water for 24 hours or nick them with a nail file before planting them. Planting a second crop of sweet peas about a month after the first one will ensure a longer blooming period. Deadhead all spent blooms.

Tips
Sweet peas will grow up poles, trellises and fences or over rocks. They cling by wrapping tendrils around their support, and therefore do best when they can cling to a rough surface, chain-link fence, small twigs or a net.

Recommended
There are many cultivars of **L. odoratus** available, though several are small and bushy rather than climbing. **'Bouquet'** is a tall, climbing variety with flowers in a wide range of colours.

Newer sweet pea cultivars often have less fragrant flowers than old-fashioned cultivars. Seek out heritage varieties for the most fragrant flowers.

Features: clinging habit, summer flowers
Flower colour: pink, red, purple, lavender, blue, salmon, pale yellow, peach, white or bicoloured **Height:** 30 cm–1.8 m (12"–6')
Spread: 15–30 cm (6–12") **Hardiness:** hardy annual

Virginia Creeper · Boston Ivy
Parthenocissus

P. quinquefolia (above & below)

Virginia creeper and Boston ivy are handsome vines that establish quickly and provide an air of age and permanence, even on new structures.

Growing

These vines grow well in any light from **full sun to full shade**. The soil should be **fertile** and **well drained**. The plants will adapt to clay or sandy soils.

Tips

Virginia creepers can cover an entire building, given enough time. They do not require support because they have clinging rootlets that adhere to just about any surface, even smooth wood, vinyl or metal. Give these plants lots of space and let them cover walls, fences or arbours.

Recommended

These two species are very similar, except for the shape of their leaves.

P. quinquefolia (Virginia creeper, woodbine) has dark green foliage. Each leaf, divided into five leaflets, turns flame red in fall.

P. tricuspidata (Boston ivy, Japanese creeper) has dark green, three-lobed leaves that turn red in fall. This species is not quite as hardy as Virginia creeper.

Features: summer and fall foliage, clinging habit
Height: 9–21 m (30–70') **Spread:** 9–21 m (30–70')
Hardiness: zones 3–8

Wisteria

Wisteria

W. sinensis (above & below)

The seeds in the long, velvety, bean-like pods, along with all parts of these plants, are poisonous.

Pruning your wisteria will allow its flower clusters to hang freely.

Loose, purple flower clusters hang like lace from the branches of wisteria.

Growing

Wisterias grow well in **full sun** or **partial shade**. The soil should be of **average fertility, moist** and **well drained**. Vines grown in too fertile a soil will produce lots of vegetative growth but very few flowers. Avoid planting wisteria near a lawn where fertilizer may leach into your vine's root zone.

Tips

Wisteria vines require something to twine around, such as an arbour or other sturdy structure. You can also stake a wisteria and train it to form a small tree. Try to select a permanent site; wisterias don't like being moved. These vigorous vines may send up suckers and can root wherever branches touch the ground. Frequent pruning will control these plants and keep them looking their best.

Recommended

W. floribunda (Japanese wisteria) bears long, pendulous clusters of fragrant blue, purple, pink or white flowers in late spring before the leaves emerge. Long, bean-like pods follow.

W. sinensis (Chinese wisteria) bears long, pendant clusters of fragrant blue-purple flowers in late spring. **'Alba'** has white flowers.

Features: late-spring flowers, foliage, twining habit **Flower colour:** white, blue, purple, pink **Height:** 6–15 m (20–50') or more **Spread:** 6–15 m (20–50') or more **Hardiness:** zones 4–8

Canna Lily
Canna

Canna lilies are stunning, dramatic plants that give an exotic flair to any garden.

Growing

Canna lilies grow best in **full sun** in a **sheltered** location. The soil should be **fertile, moist** and **well drained**. Plant them out in spring, after the last frost date and once the soil has warmed. Plants can be started early indoors in containers for a head start on the growing season. If flowers are properly deadheaded, they will continue to bloom until the first frost.

Tips

Canna lilies can be grown in a bed or border. They make dramatic specimen plants and can even be included in large planters.

Recommended

A wide range of canna lilies are available, including cultivars and hybrids with green, bronzy, purple or yellow-and-green-striped foliage. Flowers may be white, red, orange, pink, yellow or bicoloured. Dwarf cultivars that grow 45–70 cm (18–28") tall are also available.

'Red King Humbert' (below)

The rhizomes can be lifted before a heavy frost. Clean off any clinging dirt and store them in a cool, frost-free location in slightly moist peat moss. Check on them regularly through the winter and if they are starting to sprout, pot them and move them to a bright window until they can be moved outdoors.

Features: decorative foliage, summer flowers **Flower colour:** white, red, orange, pink, yellow or bicoloured **Height:** 1–2 m (3–6') **Spread:** 50–90 cm (20–36") **Hardiness:** zones 7–8; grown as an annual

Crocus

Crocus

C. x *vernus* cultivars (above & below)

Crocuses are harbingers of spring. They often appear, as if by magic, in full bloom from beneath the melting snow.

Growing

Crocuses grow well in **full sun** or **light, dappled shade**. The soil should be of **poor to average fertility, gritty** and **well drained**. The corms are planted about 10 cm (4") deep in fall. Foliage should be left in place after the plants flower, but can be cut back once it begins to wither and turn brown in summer.

Tips

Crocuses are almost always planted in groups. Drifts of crocuses in a lawn will provide interest and colour while the grass still lies dormant. After the foliage withers in mid-June, they may be mowed over. In beds and borders they can be left to naturalize. Groups of plants will fill in and spread out to provide a bright welcome in spring. Plant perennials among the crocuses to fill the gaps once the crocuses die.

Recommended

Many crocus species, hybrids and cultivars are available. The spring-flowering crocus most people are familiar with is *C.* x *vernus*, commonly called Dutch crocus. Many cultivars are available with flowers in shades of purple, yellow and white, sometimes bicoloured or with darker veins.

Features: early-spring flowers **Flower colour:** purple, yellow, white, bicoloured **Height:** 5–15 cm (2–6") **Spread:** 5–10 cm (2–4") **Hardiness:** zones 3–8

Daffodil

Narcissus

Many gardeners automatically think of large, yellow, trumpet-shaped flowers when they think of daffodils, but there is a lot of variety in colour, form and size among the daffodils.

Growing

Daffodils grow best in **full sun** or **light, dappled shade**. The soil should be **average to fertile, moist** and **well drained**. Bulbs should be planted in fall, 5–20 cm (2–8") deep, depending on the size of the bulb. The bigger the bulb, the deeper it should be planted. A rule of thumb is to measure the bulb from top to bottom and multiply that number by three to know how deep to plant. Leave the foliage in place once flowering is finished. Foliage can be cut back once the daffodils wither and turn brown.

Tips

Daffodils are often planted where they can be left to naturalize—in the light shade beneath a deciduous tree or in a woodland garden. In mixed beds and borders, the daffodils' faded leaves will be hidden by the summer foliage of other plants.

Recommended

Many species, hybrids and cultivars of daffodils are available. Flowers may be 4–15 cm (¹/₂–6") across, solitary or borne in clusters. There are 12 different flower form classifications.

The cup in the centre of a daffodil is called the corona and the group of petals that surrounds the corona is called the perianth.

Features: spring flowers **Flower colour:** white, yellow, peach, orange, light pink; may be bicoloured **Height:** 10–60 cm (4–24")
Spread: 10–30 cm (4–12")
Hardiness: zones 3–8

Dahlia

Dahlia

Mixed cutting bed (above)

The variation in size, shape and colour of dahlia flowers is astonishing. You are sure to find at least one of these old-fashioned but popular plants that appeals to you.

Growing

Dahlias prefer **full sun**. The soil should be **fertile,** rich in **organic matter, moist** and **well drained**. All dahlias are tender, tuberous perennials treated as annuals. Tubers can be purchased and started early indoors. They can also be lifted in fall and stored over winter in slightly moist peat moss. Pot the tubers and keep them in a bright room after they start sprouting in mid- to late winter. Deadhead to keep plants tidy and blooming.

Tips

Dahlias make attractive, colourful additions to a mixed border. The smaller varieties make good edging plants and the larger ones are good alternatives to shrubs. Varieties with unusual or interesting flowers are attractive specimen plants.

Recommended

Of the many dahlia hybrids, most are grown from tubers but a few can be started from seed. Many hybrids are classified and sold based on flower shape, such as collarette (single), decorative (double) or peony-flowered. The flowers range in size from 5–30 cm (2–12") and are available in many shades. The foliage is decorative too, ranging in colour from bright green to bronze to purple. Check with your local garden centre to see what is available.

Features: summer to fall flowers, attractive foliage, bushy habit **Flower colour:** shades of purple, pink, white, yellow, orange, red; some bicoloured **Height:** 20 cm–1.5 m (8"–5') **Spread:** 20–45 cm (8–18") **Hardiness:** tender perennial grown as an annual

Flowering Onion

Allium

*F*lowering onions, with their striking, ball-like or loose clusters of flowers, are sure to attract attention in the garden.

Growing

Flowering onions grow best in **full sun**. The soil should be **average to fertile, moist** and **well drained**. Plant bulbs in fall, 5–10 cm (2–4") deep, depending on the size of the bulb.

Tips

Flowering onions are best planted in groups in a bed or border where they can be left to naturalize. Most will self-seed when left to their own devices. The foliage, which tends to fade just as the plants come into flower, can be hidden with perennials, groundcovers or a low, bushy companion plant.

Recommended

Several flowering onion species, hybrids and cultivars have gained popularity for their decorative flowers. These include *A. aflatunense*, with dense, globe-like clusters of lavender flowers; *A. caeruleum* (blue globe onion), with globe-like clusters of blue flowers; *A. cernuum* (nodding or wild onion), with loose, drooping clusters of pink flowers; *A. giganteum* (giant onion), a big plant up to 1.2 m (4') tall, with large, globe-shaped clusters of pinky lavender flowers; and *A. sphaerocephalum* (round-headed leek, drumstick allium), with single, egg-shaped clusters of burgundy flowers.

A. giganteum (above), A. cernuum (below)

Though flowering onion leaves have an onion scent when bruised, the flowers are often sweetly fragrant.

Features: summer flowers, cylindrical or strap-shaped leaves **Flower colour:** pink, purple, white, yellow, blue, maroon, lavender, burgundy **Height:** 30 cm–1.2 m (12"–4') **Spread:** 5–30 cm (2–12") **Hardiness:** zones 3–8

Gladiolus
Gladiolus

'Homecoming' (below)

Perhaps best known as a cut flower, gladiolus adds an air of extravagance to the garden.

Growing

Gladiolus grows best in **full sun** but tolerates partial shade. The soil should be **fertile, humus rich, moist** and **well drained**. Flower spikes may need staking and a sheltered location out of the wind to prevent them from blowing over.

Plant corms in spring, 10–15 cm (4–6") deep, once soil has warmed. Corms can also be started early indoors. Plant a few corms each week for about a month to prolong the blooming period.

Tips

Planted in groups in beds and borders, gladiolus makes a bold statement. Corms can also be pulled up in fall and stored in damp peat moss in a cool, frost-free location for the winter.

Recommended

Gladiolus hybrids have flowers that come in almost every imaginable shade, except blue. Plants are commonly grouped in three classifications: **Grandiflorus** is the best known; each corm produces a single spike of large, often ruffled flowers; **Nanus**, the hardiest group, survives in zone 3 with protection and produces several spikes of up to seven flowers. **Primulinus** produces a single spike of up to 23 flowers that grow more spaced out than those of the grandiflorus.

Features: brightly coloured, mid- to late-summer flowers **Flower colour:** almost every colour except blue **Height:** 45 cm–1.8 m (18"–6') **Spread:** 15–30 cm (6–12") **Hardiness:** zone 8; grown as an annual

Lily
Lilium

Decorative clusters of large, richly coloured blooms grace these tall plants. Flowers are produced at differing times of the season, depending on the hybrid. With the proper cultivars, it is possible to have lilies blooming all season.

Growing

Lilies grow best in **full sun** but like to have their **roots shaded**. The soil should be rich in **organic matter, fertile, moist** and **well drained**. Lilies should be planted deep in the soil. Plant the smaller bulbs 10 cm (4") deep and the large ones 20 cm (8") deep.

Tips

Lilies are often grouped in beds and borders and can be naturalized in woodland gardens and near water features. These plants are narrow but tall; plant at least three together to make a statement.

Recommended

The many lily species, hybrids and cultivars available are grouped by type. Visit your local garden centre to see what is available. The following are two popular groups of lilies. **Asiatic hybrids** bear clusters of flowers in early summer or mid-summer and are available in a wide range of colours. **Oriental hybrids** bear clusters of large, fragrant flowers in mid- and late summer. Colours are usually white, pink or red.

Asiatic hybrids (above), 'Stargazer' (below)

Lily bulbs should be planted in fall before the first frost, but they can also be planted in spring if bulbs are available. Garden centres often start lilies in pots, ready to be planted into the garden.

Also called: asiatic lily, oriental lily **Features:** early-, mid- or late-season flowers **Flower colour:** shades of orange, yellow, peach, pink, purple, red, white **Height:** 60 cm–1.5 m (2–5') **Spread:** 30 cm (12") **Hardiness:** zones 4–8

Tulip

Tulipa

Tulips, with their beautiful, often garishly coloured flowers are a welcome sight as we enjoy the warm days of spring.

Growing

Tulips grow best in **full sun**. The flowers tend to bend toward the light in partial or light shade. The soil should be **fertile** and **well drained**. Plant bulbs in fall, 15 cm (6") deep, depending on the size of the bulb. Although tulips can repeat bloom, many hybrids perform best if planted new each year. Species and older cultivars are the best choice for naturalizing.

During the tulipomania of the 1630s, the bulbs were worth many times their weight in gold. Many tulip speculators lost massive fortunes when the mania ended.

Tips

Tulips provide the best display when mass planted or planted in groups in flowerbeds and borders. They can also be grown in containers and forced to bloom early in pots indoors. Some of the species and older cultivars can be naturalized in meadow and wildflower gardens.

Tulip flowers are edible. Remove the stamens and pistil, then fill the flower with a herbed cream cheese or egg spread.

Recommended

There are about 100 species of tulips and thousands of hybrids and cultivars, generally divided into 15 groups based on bloom time and flower appearance. They come in dozens of shades, including bicoloured and multi-coloured. Blue is the only shade not available. Check your local garden centre or mail-order catalogue in early fall for the best selection.

Features: spring flowers **Flower colour:** any shade except blue **Height:** 15–75 cm (6–30") **Spread:** 5–20 cm (2–8") **Hardiness:** zones 3–8; often treated as an annual

Basil
Ocimum

O. basilicum 'Red Rubin' (above), *O. b.* 'Genovese' (below)

The sweet, fragrant leaves of fresh basil add a delicious licorice-like flavour to salads and tomato-based dishes.

Growing

Basil grows best in a **warm, sheltered** location in **full sun**. The soil should be **fertile, moist** and **well drained**. Pinch off tips and flowers regularly to encourage bushy growth and lots of leaves. Plant out or direct sow seed after frost danger has passed in spring.

Tips

Though basil grows best outdoors in a warm spot in the garden, it can be grown successfully indoors, in a pot by a bright window, to provide you with fresh leaves all year.

Recommended

O. basilicum is one of the most popular culinary herbs, with dozens of varieties, sizes, colours and flavours. **'Genovese'** is a green-leaved variety. **'Lesbos'** has a distinct, spicy flavour; **'Mammoth'** has large leaves while **'Minimum'** has smooth foliage. **'Purple Ruffles,'** in contrast, has ruffled leaves; **'Red Robin's'** leaves are purple; and **'Spicy Globe's'** are tiny. **'Sweet Dani'** is known for its lemony flavour. Thai flavours are also available.

Features: fragrant, decorative leaves **Height:** 30–60 cm (12–24") **Spread:** 30–45 cm (12–18") **Hardiness:** tender annual

Chives
Allium

A. *schoenoprasum* (above & below)

Chives' delicate onion flavour is best enjoyed fresh, but this herb can be stored frozen. Mix chives into dips or sprinkle them on salads and baked potatoes.

Growing
Chives grow best in **full sun**. The soil should be **fertile, moist** and **well drained**, but chives adapt to most soil conditions. These plants are easy to start from seed, but they will wait until the soil temperature remains above 19° C (66° F) before they germinate. Seeds started directly in

The edible flowers bring colour to a salad.

the garden are, therefore, unlikely to sprout before early summer.

Tips
Chives look decorative enough to include in a mixed or herbaceous border, and they can be left to naturalize. In a herb garden, chives should be given plenty of space to allow self-seeding. Deadheading will reduce self-seeding.

Recommended
A. schoenoprasum forms a clump of bright green, cylindrical leaves. Clusters of pinky purple flowers are produced in early and mid-summer. Varieties with white or pink flowers are also available.

A. tuberosum (garlic chives, Chinese chives) forms a clump of narrow, strap-like leaves that have a mild garlic flavour. Clusters of white, star-like flowers are produced in early and mid-summer.

Features: foliage, form, flowers **Height:** 20–60 cm (8–24") **Spread:** 30 cm (12") or more **Hardiness:** zones 3–8

Coriander · Cilantro

Coriandrum

Coriander is a multi-purpose herb. The leaves, called cilantro, can be added to salads, salsas and soups. The seeds, called coriander, are used in pies, chutneys and marmalades.

Growing

Coriander prefers **full sun** but tolerates partial shade. The soil should be **fertile, light** and **well drained**. These plants dislike humid conditions and grow best during dry summers.

Tips

Coriander has pungent leaves and is best planted where people will not have to brush past it. It is, however, a delight to behold in flower. Add coriander plants here and there throughout your borders and vegetable garden. They will create visual appeal and attract pollinators such as bees and butterflies, as well as beneficial insects that deter pest insects.

Recommended

C. sativum forms a clump of lacy basal foliage, similar in appearance to flat-leaf parsley, followed by stalks bearing finely divided, dill-like leaves and terminating in loose clusters of tiny, white flowers. The seeds ripen in late summer and fall and should be harvested before they shatter.

Basal leaves (above), upper leaves (below)

Cilantro goes to seed quickly, especially in hot weather. Pinch stalks back as they appear, and sow seeds every week or so in spring and early summer to prolong leaf production.

Features: form, foliage, flowers, seeds
Height: 40–60 cm (16–24") **Spread:** 20–40 cm (8–16") **Hardiness:** tender annual

Dill

Anethum

A. graveolens (above & below)

Dill leaves and seeds are probably best known for their use as pickling herbs, though they have a wide variety of other culinary uses and are a popular accompaniment to seafood.

Growing

Dill grows best in **full sun,** in a **sheltered** location out of strong winds. The soil should be of **poor to average fertility, moist** and **well drained**. Sow seeds every couple of weeks in spring and early summer to ensure a regular supply of leaves. Plants should not be grown near fennel; they will cross-pollinate and the seeds will lose their distinct flavours. Use twiggy branches to stake tall plants when they are young. This will prevent them from flopping over when they mature.

Tips

With its feathery leaves, dill makes an attractive addition to a mixed bed or border. It can be included in a vegetable garden but does well in any sunny location. It also attracts predatory insects to the garden. Pinching out flowering tips will encourage leaf production but will also prevent seed formation.

To collect the seeds, cut off the seedheads before they ripen and keep them in a paper bag in a warm, dry place.

Recommended

A. graveolens forms a clump of feathery foliage. Clusters of yellow flowers are borne on top of sturdy stems. Cultivars are available, including **'Fernleaf,'** a compact dwarf plant that is slow to flower and doesn't require staking.

Features: feathery, edible foliage; yellow summer flowers; edible seeds **Height:** 60 cm–1.5 m (24"–5') **Spread:** 30 cm (12") or more **Hardiness:** annual

Mint
Mentha

Mint's cool, refreshing flavour makes it a good decorative garnish and addition to tea and other hot or cold beverages. Mint sauce, made from freshly chopped leaves, is often served with lamb.

Growing

Mint grows well in **full sun and partial shade**. The soil should be **average to fertile, humus rich** and **moist**. These plants spread by rhizomes and may need a barrier in the soil or some other contained location to restrict their spread.

Tips

Mint is often vigorously invasive; place it where it can be contained to prevent it from overwhelming less vigorous plants. It makes a useful groundcover for difficult sites where little else will grow.

The flowers attract bees, butterflies and other pollinators to the garden.

Recommended

Mint has many species, hybrids and cultivars. Peppermint (**M. x piperita**), orange mint (**M. x piperita citrata**) and spearmint (**M. spicata**) are three of the most commonly grown culinary varieties. There are also more decorative varieties with variegated or curly leaves, as well as varieties with unusual, fruit-scented leaves.

M. x piperita (above), *M. x gracilis* 'Variegata' (below)

A few sprigs of fresh mint added to a pitcher of iced tea gives it an added zip.

Features: summer flowers, fragrant foliage
Flower colour: purple, pink, white **Height:** 15–90 cm (6–36") **Spread:** 90 cm (36") or more **Hardiness:** zones 4–8

Oregano · Marjoram
Origanum

O. vulgare hirtum 'Polyphant' (above), *O. v. h.* 'Aureum' (below)

Oregano and marjoram are two of the best-known and most frequently used herbs. They are popular in stuffings, soups and stews, and no pizza is complete until it has been sprinkled with fresh or dried oregano leaves.

Growing

Oregano and marjoram grow best in **full sun**. The soil should be of **poor to average fertility, neutral to alkaline** and **well drained**. The flowers attract pollinators to the garden.

Tips

These bushy perennials make lovely additions to any border and can be trimmed to form low hedges. They spread aggressively, but well-behaved cultivars with ornamental spreading, trailing and flowering characteristics are available.

Recommended

O. majorana (marjoram) is upright and shrubby with light green, hairy leaves and a sweeter, more delicate flavour than oregano. It bears white or pink flowers in summer and can be grown as an annual in areas where it is not hardy.

O. vulgare hirtum (oregano, Greek oregano) is the most flavourful culinary variety of oregano. This low, bushy plant has hairy, grey-green leaves and bears white flowers. Many other interesting varieties of *O. vulgare* are available, including some with golden, variegated or curly leaves.

Features: fragrant foliage, summer flowers, bushy habit **Flower colour:** white, pink **Height:** 30–80 cm (12–32") **Spread:** 20–45 cm (8–18") **Hardiness:** zones 5–8

Parsley
Petroselinum

P. crispum (above & below)

Though usually used as a garnish, parsley is rich in vitamins and minerals and is reputed to freshen the breath after garlic- or onion-rich foods are eaten.

Growing

Parsley grows well in **full sun** or **partial shade**. The soil should be of **average to rich fertility, humus rich, moist** and **well drained**. Direct sow seeds; these plants resent transplanting. If you start seeds early, use peat pots so the plants can be potted or planted out without disruption.

Tips

Parsley should be started where you intend to grow it. Containers of parsley can be kept close to the house for easy picking. Its bright green leaves and compact growth habit make parsley a good edging plant for beds and borders. Its colour and texture will contrast nicely with other foliage and flowers.

Recommended

P. crispum forms a clump of bright green, divided leaves. This plant is biennial, flowering in its second summer, but it grows best when treated as an annual. Cultivars may have flat or curly leaves. Flat leaves have more flavour and curly leaves are more decorative. Dwarf and extra curly cultivars are also available.

If you see a yellow, black and white caterpillar feeding on your parsley, leave it be; it is the larvae of the black swallowtail butterfly.

Features: attractive foliage **Height:** 20–60 cm (8–24") **Spread:** 30–60 cm (12–24")
Hardiness: zones 5–8; grown as an annual

Rosemary
Rosmarinus

Rosemary's needle-like leaves are used to flavour a wide variety of culinary dishes, including chicken, pork, lamb, rice, tomato, potato and egg dishes.

Growing

Rosemary prefers **full sun** but tolerates partial shade. The soil should be of **poor to average fertility** and **well drained**. Place it in an area with good air circulation to prevent mildew.

Tips

In Ontario, rosemary is usually grown in a container as a specimen or with other plants, but you can grow it in a shrub border where it's hardy. Low-growing, spreading plants can be included in a rock garden, along the top of a retaining wall, or in hanging baskets and containers. Plants can also be trained into standard forms and trimmed to form topiary shapes.

Recommended

R. officinalis is a dense, bushy, tender evergreen shrub with narrow, dark green leaves. The habit varies somewhat between cultivars, from strongly upright to prostrate and spreading. Flowers usually come in shades of blue, but pink- or white-flowered cultivars are available. A cultivar called **'Arp'** can survive in zone 6 in a sheltered location with winter protection. Plants rarely reach their mature size when grown in containers.

Rosemary makes a nice standard (above), *R. officinalis* (below)

To overwinter a container-grown plant, keep it in very light or partial shade in summer, then put it in a sunny window indoors during the winter. Keep it well watered, but allow it to dry out slightly between waterings.

Features: fragrant evergreen foliage, summer flowers
Flower colour: usually bright blue, sometimes pink or white **Height:** 20 cm–1.2 m (8"–4') **Spread:** 30 cm–1.2 m (12"–4') **Hardiness:** zone 8

Sage
Salvia

Sage is perhaps best known as a flavouring for stuffing, but it has a great range of uses, including in soups, stews, sausages and dumplings.

Growing

Sage prefers **full sun** but tolerates light shade. The soil should be of **average fertility** and **well drained**. These plants benefit from a light mulch of compost each year. They are drought tolerant once established.

Tips

Sage is an attractive ornamental herb for the border. It adds volume to the middle of a border and makes an attractive edging or feature plant for foliage contrast. Sage can also be grown in mixed planters. Harvest the leaves any time during the summer, and use them fresh or dried.

Recommended

S. officinalis is a woody, mounding plant with soft, grey-green leaves. Spikes of light purple flowers appear in early and mid-summer, though not all cultivars will flower in Ontario. Many cultivars with attractive foliage are available, but they are usually only hardy to zone 6. These include the silver-leaved **'Berggarten,'** the yellow-margined **'Icterina,'** the purple new-leaved **'Purpurascens'** and the purple, green and cream variegated **'Tricolor,'** which has a pink flush to its new growth.

S. officinalis 'Icterina' (above), *S. o.* 'Purpurascens' (below)

Sage is reputed to deter cabbage moths, making it a good companion plant for the vegetable garden.

Features: fragrant, decorative foliage; summer flowers **Flower colour:** blue, purple **Height:** 30–60 cm (12–24") **Spread:** 45–90 cm (18–36") **Hardiness:** zones 5–8

Thyme
Thymus

T. serpyllum (above), T. x citriodorus 'Argenteus' (below)

These plants are bee and butterfly magnets when in bloom.

Thyme is a popular culinary herb used in soups, stews, casseroles and with roasts.

Growing

Thyme prefers **full sun**. The soil should be **neutral to alkaline** and of **poor to average fertility. Good drainage** is essential. Work leaf mould and sharp limestone gravel into the soil to improve structure and drainage.

Tips

Plant thyme in sunny, dry locations at the front of borders, between or beside paving stones, on rock gardens and rock walls and in containers.

Once the plants have finished flowering, shear them back by about half to encourage new growth and prevent the plants from becoming too woody.

Recommended

T. x citriodorus (lemon-scented thyme) forms a mound of lemon-scented, dark green foliage. It is only hardy to zone 6. The flowers are pale pink. Cultivars with silver- or gold-margined leaves are available.

T. vulgaris (common thyme) forms a bushy mound of dark green leaves and is the species most commonly used for flavouring. The flowers may be purple, pink or white. Cultivars with variegated leaves are available.

Features: bushy habit; fragrant, decorative foliage; flowers **Flower colour:** purple, pink, white **Height:** 20–40 cm (8–16") **Spread:** 20–40 cm (8–16") **Hardiness:** zones 4–8

Fescue
Festuca

F. glauca 'Elijah Blue' (above), *F. glauca* (below)

This fine-leaved ornamental grass forms tufted clumps that resemble pin cushions. Their metallic blue colouring adds an all-season cooling accent to the garden.

Growing

Fescue thrives in **full sun** to **light shade**. The soil should be of **average fertility**, **moist** and **well drained**. The plants are **drought tolerant** once established. Fescue emerges early in the spring, so shear it back to 2.5 cm (1") above the crown in late winter, before new growth emerges. Shear off flower stalks just above the foliage to keep the plant tidy or to prevent self seeding.

Tips

With its fine texture and distinct blue colour, this grass can be used as a single specimen in a rock garden or a container planting. Plant fescue in drifts to create a sea of blue or a handsome edge to a bed, border or pathway. It looks attractive in both formal and informal gardens.

Recommended

F. glauca (blue fescue) forms tidy, tufted clumps of fine, blue-toned foliage and panicles of flowers in May and June. Cultivars and hybrids come in varying heights and in shades ranging from blue to olive green. **'Boulder Blue,' 'Elijah Blue,' 'Skinner's Blue'** and **'Solling'** are popular selections.

Also called: blue fescue **Features:** blue to blue-green foliage, colour that persists into winter, habit **Height:** 15–30 cm (6–12")
Spread: 25–30 cm (10–12")
Hardiness: zones 3–8

Flowering Fern
Osmunda

O. regalis (above & below)

The flowering fern's 'flowers' are actually its spore-producing sporangia.

Ferns have a certain prehistoric mystique, and they can add a graceful elegance and textural accent to the garden.

Growing
Flowering ferns prefer **light shade** but tolerate full sun if the soil is consistently moist. The soil should **be fertile, humus rich, acidic** and **moist**. Flowering ferns tolerate wet soil and will spread as offsets form at the plant bases.

Tips
These large ferns form an attractive mass when planted in large colonies. They can be included in beds and borders, and make a welcome addition to a woodland garden.

Recommended
O. cinnamomea (cinnamon fern) has light green fronds that fan out in a circular fashion from a central point. Bright green, leafless fertile fronds that mature to cinnamon brown are produced in spring and stand straight up in the centre of the plant. (Zones 2–8)

O. regalis (royal fern) forms a dense clump of foliage. Feathery, flower-like fertile fronds stand out among the sterile fronds in summer and mature to a rusty brown. **'Purpurascens'** fronds are purple-red when they emerge in spring and then mature to green. This contrasts well with the purple stems. (Zones 3–8)

Features: perennial, deciduous fern; decorative fertile fronds; habit **Height:** 75 cm–1.5 m (30"–5') **Spread:** 60–90 cm (2–3') **Hardiness:** zones 2–8

Fountain Grass

Pennisetum

Fountain grass' low maintenance and graceful form make it easy to place. It will soften any landscape, even in winter.

Growing

Fountain grass thrives in **full sun**. The soil should be of **average fertility** and **well drained**. These plants are drought tolerant once established. They may self-seed, but are not troublesome. Shear perennials back in early spring, and divide them when they start to die out in the centre.

Tips

Fountain grasses can be used as individual specimen plants, in group plantings and drifts or combined with flowering annuals, perennials, shrubs and other ornamental grasses. Annual selections are often planted in containers or beds for height and stature.

Recommended

Both perennial and annual fountain grasses exist. Popular perennials include *P. alopecuroides* **'Hameln'** (dwarf perennial fountain grass), a compact cultivar with silvery white plumes and narrow, dark green foliage that turns gold in fall (zones 5–8) and *P. orientale* (Oriental fountain grass), with tall, blue-green foliage and large, silvery white flowers (zones 6–8, with winter protection).

Annual fountain grasses include *P. setaceum* (annual fountain grass) has narrow, green foliage and pinkish purple

P. setaceum 'Rubrum' (above & below)

flowers that mature to grey. Its cultivar **'Rubrum'** (red annual fountain grass) has broader, deep burgundy foliage and pinkish purple flowers. *P. glaucum* **'Purple Majesty'** (purple ornamental millet) has blackish purple foliage and coarse, bottlebrush flowers. Its form resembles a corn stalk.

The name Pennisetum alopecuroides *refers to its plumy flower spikes, which resemble a fox's tail. In Latin,* penna *means feather and* seta *means bristle;* alopekos *is the Greek word for fox.*

Features: arching, fountain-like or upright habit; silvery pink, dusty rose to purplish black foliage; flowers; winter interest **Height:** 60 cm–1.5 m (2–5') **Spread:** 60–90 cm (2–3') **Hardiness:** zones 5–8 or grown as an annual

Maidenhair Fern

Adiantum

A. pedatum (above & below)

These charming and delicate-looking native ferns add a graceful touch to a woodland planting. Their unique habit and texture will stand out in any garden.

Growing

Maidenhair fern grows well in **light shade** or **partial shade** and tolerates full shade.

Try growing the fine-textured and delicate maidenhair fern with hostas, lungwort and Siberian bugloss. It will create a nice contrast in texture.

The soil should be of **average fertility, humus rich, slightly acidic** and **moist**. This plant rarely needs dividing, but it can be divided in spring to propagate more plants.

Tips

These lovely ferns will do well in any shaded spot in the garden. Include them in rock gardens, woodland gardens, shaded borders and beneath shade trees. They also make attractive additions to a shaded planting next to a water feature or on a slope where the foliage can be seen when it sways in the breeze.

Recommended

A. pedatum forms a spreading mound of delicate, arching fronds. Light green leaflets stand out against the black stems, and the whole plant turns bright yellow in fall. Spores are produced on the undersides of the leaflets.

Also called: northern maidenhair
Features: deciduous perennial fern, summer and fall foliage, habit **Height:** 30–60 cm (12–24") **Spread:** 30–60 cm (12–24")
Hardiness: zones 2–8

Miscanthus
Miscanthus

Miscanthus is one of the most popular and majestic of all the ornamental grasses. Its graceful foliage dances in the wind and makes an impressive sight all year long.

Growing
Miscanthus prefers **full sun**. The soil should be of **average fertility**, **moist** and **well drained,** though some selections also tolerate wet soil. All selections are drought tolerant once established.

Tips
Give these magnificent beauties room to spread so you can fully appreciate their form. The plant's height will determine the best place for each selection in the border. They create dramatic impact in groups or as seasonal screens.

Recommended
M. **'Purparescens'** (flame grass), has foliage that turns bright orange in early fall. There are many available cultivars of *M. sinensis*, all distinguished by a white midrib on the leaf blade. Some popular selections include **'Gracillimus'** (maiden grass), with long, fine-textured leaves; **'Grosse Fontaine'** (large fountain), a tall, wide-spreading, early-flowering selection; **'Morning Light'** (variegated maiden grass), a shorter and more delicate plant with fine, white leaf edges; and **'Strictus'** (porcupine grass), a tall, stiff, upright selection with unusual horizontal yellow bands.

M. sinensis 'Grosse Fontaine' (above), *M. s.* 'Zebrinus' (below)

An Ontario plant breeder named Martin Quinn introduced many miscanthus selections. These attractive cultivars have names such as 'Huron Sunrise,' 'Huron Sunset' and 'Huron Blush' to reflect their place of origin: Kincardine, on the shore of Lake Huron.

Also called: eulalia, Japanese silver grass
Features: upright, arching habit; colourful summer and fall foliage; late-summer and fall flowers; winter interest **Flower colour:** pink, copper, silver **Height:** 1.2–2.4 m (4–8')
Spread: 60 cm–1.2m (2–4')
Hardiness: zones 5–8, possibly zone 4

Ostrich Fern
Matteuccia

M. struthiopteris (above & below)

These popular classic ferns are revered for their delicious, emerging spring fronds and their stately, vase-shaped habits.

Growing
Ostrich fern prefers **partial** or **light shade** but tolerates full shade and even full sun if the soil is kept moist. The soil should be **average to fertile**, **humus rich**, **neutral to acidic** and **moist**. The leaves may scorch if soil is not moist enough. These ferns are aggressive spreaders that reproduce by spores. Unwanted plants can be pulled up and composted or given away.

Tips
This fern appreciates a moist woodland garden and is often found growing wild alongside woodland streams and creeks. Useful in shaded borders, these plants are quick to spread, to the delight of those who enjoy the young fronds as a culinary delicacy.

Recommended
M. struthiopteris forms a circular cluster of slightly arching, feathery fronds. Stiff, brown, fertile fronds, covered in reproductive spores, stick up in the centre of the cluster in late summer and persist through the winter. These are popular choices for dried arrangements.

Ostrich ferns are also grown commercially for their edible fiddleheads. The tightly coiled, new spring fronds taste delicious lightly steamed and served with butter. Remove the bitter, reddish brown, papery coating before steaming.

Also called: fiddlehead fern **Features:** perennial fern, foliage, habit **Height:** 90 cm–1.5 m (3–5') **Spread:** 30–90 cm (12–36") or more **Hardiness:** zones 1–8

Pachysandra
Pachysandra

P. terminalis (above & below)

Low-maintenance pachysandra is one of the most popular groundcovers. Its rhizomatous rootzone colonizes quickly to form a dense blanket over the ground.

Growing

Pachysandra prefers **light to full shade**. Any soil that is **moist, acidic, humus rich** and **well drained** is good. These plants can be propagated easily from cuttings or by division.

Tips

Pachysandras are durable groundcovers under trees, in shady borders and in woodland gardens. The foliage is considered evergreen, but winter-scorched shoots may need to be removed in spring. Shear or mow old plantings in early spring to rejuvenate them.

Recommended

P. terminalis (Japanese Spurge) forms a low mass of foliage rosettes. It grows about 20 cm (8") tall and can spread almost indefinitely. **'Green Sheen'** has, as its name implies, exceptionally glossy leaves that are smaller than those of the species. **'Variegata'** has white margins or mottled silver foliage, but it is not as vigorous as the species.

Interplant this popular groundcover with spring bulbs, hostas or ferns, or use it as an underplanting for deciduous trees and shrubs with contrasting foliage colours.

Also called: Japanese spurge
Features: perennial, evergreen groundcover; habit; inconspicuous, fragrant, white, spring flowers **Height:** 20 cm (8") **Spread:** 30–45 cm (12–18") or more **Hardiness:** zones 3–8

Reed Grass

Calamagrostis

C. x acutiflora 'Karl Foerster' (above & below)

If you like how reed grass holds its flowers high above its mounded foliage, consider Deschampsia (tufted hair grass) and Molinia (moor grass) and their species and cultivars. Some have creamy yellow striped foliage.

This is a graceful, metamorphic grass that changes its habit and flower colour throughout the seasons. The slightest breeze keeps this grass in perpetual motion.

Growing

Reed grass grows best in **full sun**. The soil should be **fertile, moist** and **well drained**, though heavy clay and dry soils are tolerated. Reed grass may be susceptible to rust in cool, wet summers or in areas with poor air circulation. Rain and heavy snow may cause it to flop temporarily, but it quickly bounces back. Cut it back to 5–10 cm (2–4") in very early spring before growth begins. Divide it if it begins to die out in the centre.

Tips

Whether it's used as a single, stately focal point, in small groupings or in large drifts, this is a desirable, low-maintenance grass. It combines well with perennials that bloom in late summer and fall.

Recommended

C. x *acutiflora* **'Karl Foerster'** (Foerster's feather reed grass), the most popular selection, forms a loose mound of green foliage from which the airy bottlebrush flowers emerge in June. The flowering stems have a loose, arching habit when they first emerge, but grow more stiff and upright over the summer. Watch for a new introduction called **'Avalanche,'** which has a wide white centre stripe. Other cultivars include **'Overdam,'** a compact, less hardy selection with white leaf edges.

Features: open habit becomes upright, silvery pink flowers turn rich tan, green foliage turns bright gold in fall, winter interest
Height: 90 cm–1.5 m (3–5') **Spread:** 60–90 cm (2–3') **Hardiness:** zones 4–8

Sea Oats
Chasmanthium

C. latifolium (above & below)

This native grass is at home in moist, shady woodlands, but its bamboo-like foliage gives it a tropical flair.

Growing

Sea oats thrives in **full shade to full sun**, although it must stay moist in full sun to avoid leaf scorch. Soil should be **fertile** and **moist**, although dry soils are tolerated. The upright, cascading habit relaxes in deep shade. It vigorously self-seeds, but the seedlings are easily removed and composted or shared with friends. Divide to control the rapid spread. Cut this plant back each spring to 5 cm (2") above the ground.

Tips

Sea oats are tremendous plants for moist, shady areas. Their upright to cascading habit, when in full bloom, makes an attractive planting alongside a stream or pond, in a large drift or in a container.

Recommended

C. latifolium forms a spreading clump of unique, bright green, bamboo-like foliage. The scaly, dangling spikelet flowers arrange themselves nicely on delicate stems just slightly above the foliage. The foliage and flowers turns bronze-gold in the fall.

Also known as: northern sea oats
Features: bamboo-like foliage, unusual flowers, winter interest **Height:** 80 cm–1.2 m (32"–4')
Spread: 45–60 cm (18–24")
Hardiness: zones 5–8

Sensitive Fern

Onoclea

O. sensibilis (above & below)

A common sight along stream banks and in wooded areas of Ontario, this native fern thrives in moist and shaded conditions.

Growing

Sensitive fern grows best in **light shade** but tolerates full shade and partial shade. The fronds can scorch if exposed to too much sun. The soil should be **fertile, humus rich** and **moist**, though some drought is tolerated. These plants are sensitive to frost and can be easily damaged by late and early frosts.

Tips

Sensitive ferns like to live in damp, shady places. Include them in shaded borders, woodland gardens and other locations with protection from the wind.

Recommended

O. sensibilis forms a mass of light green, deeply lobed, arching fronds. Fertile fronds are produced in late summer and persist through the winter. The spores are produced in structures that look like black beads, which give the fertile fronds a decorative appearance that makes them a popular addition to floral arrangements. The tightly coiled spring shoots (fiddleheads) are edible.

Features: deciduous perennial fern, attractive foliage, habit **Height:** 60 cm (24") **Spread:** indefinite **Hardiness:** zones 4–8

Sweet Woodruff

Galium

G. odoratum (above & below)

Sweet Woodruff is a groundcover with abundant good qualities: attractive, light green foliage that smells like new-mown hay; profuse, white spring flowers; and the ability to fill garden spaces without taking over.

Growing

This plant prefers **partial shade**. It will grow well, but will not bloom well, in full shade. Soil should be **humus rich, slightly acidic** and **evenly moist**. Sweet woodruff competes well with other plant roots and does well where some other groundcovers, like vinca, fail to thrive.

Tips

Sweet woodruff makes a perfect woodland groundcover. It forms a beautiful, green carpet and loves the same conditions in which azaleas and rhododendrons thrive. Interplant it with spring bulbs for a fantastic display in spring.

Recommended

G. odoratum is a low, spreading groundcover. It bears clusters of star-shaped, white flowers in a flush in late spring, and these continue to appear sporadically through mid-summer.

Features: deciduous perennial groundcover; white, late-spring to mid-summer flowers; fragrant foliage; habit **Height:** 30–45 cm (12–18") **Spread:** indefinite **Hardiness:** zones 3–8

Switch Grass

Panicum

P. v. 'Heavy Metal' (above & below)

Switch grass' delicate, airy panicles fill gaps in the garden border and can be cut for fresh or dried arrangements.

A native of the prairie grasslands, switch grass naturalizes equally well in an informal border and a natural meadow.

Growing

Switch grass thrives in **full sun, light shade** and **part shade**. The soil should be of **average fertility** and **well drained**, though plants adapt to both moist and dry soils and tolerate conditions ranging from heavy clay to lighter sandy soil. Cut them back to 5–10 cm (2–4") from the ground in early spring. The flower stems may break under heavy, wet snow or in exposed, windy sites.

Tips

Plant switch grass singly in small gardens, in large groups in spacious borders or at the edges of ponds or pools for a dramatic, whimsical effect. The seedheads attract birds and the foliage changes colour in the fall, so place this plant where you can enjoy both features.

Recommended

P. virgatum (switch grass) is suited to wild meadow gardens. Some of its popular cultivars include **'Heavy Metal'** (blue switch grass), an upright plant with narrow, steely blue foliage flushed with gold and burgundy in fall; **'Prairie Sky'** (blue switch grass), an arching plant with deep blue foliage; and **'Shenandoah'** (red switch grass), with red-tinged, green foliage that turns burgundy in fall.

Features: clumping habit; green, blue or burgundy foliage; airy panicles of flowers; fall colour; winter interest **Height:** 90 cm–1.5 m (3–5') **Spread:** 75–90 cm (30–36") **Hardiness:** zones 3–8

Glossary

Acid soil: soil with a pH lower than 7.0

Annual: a plant that germinates, flowers, sets seed and dies in one growing season

Alkaline soil: soil with a pH higher than 7.0

Basal leaves: leaves that form from the crown, at the base of the plant

Bract: a modified leaf at the base of a flower or flower cluster

Corm: a bulb-like, food-storing, underground stem, resembling a bulb without scales

Crown: the part of the plant at or just below soil level where the shoots join the roots

Cultivar: a cultivated plant variety with one or more distinct differences from the species, e.g., in flower colour or disease resistance

Damping off: fungal disease causing seedlings to rot at soil level and topple over

Deadhead: to remove spent flowers to maintain a neat appearance and encourage a longer blooming season

Direct sow: to sow seeds directly in the garden

Dormancy: a period of plant inactivity, usually during winter or unfavourable conditions

Double flower: a flower with an unusually large number of petals

Genus: a category of biological classification between the species and family levels; the first word in a scientific name indicates the genus

Grafting: a type of propagation in which a stem or bud of one plant is joined onto the rootstock of another plant of a closely related species

Hardy: capable of surviving unfavourable conditions, such as cold weather or frost, without protection

Hip: the fruit of a rose, containing the seeds

Humus: decomposed or decomposing organic material in the soil

Hybrid: a plant resulting from natural or human-induced cross-breeding between varieties, species or genera

Inflorescence: a flower cluster

Neutral soil: soil with a pH of 7.0

Perennial: a plant that takes three or more years to complete its life cycle

pH: a measure of acidity or alkalinity; the soil pH influences availability of nutrients for plants

Rhizome: a root-like, food-storing stem that grows horizontally at or just below soil level, from which new shoots may emerge

Rootball: the root mass and surrounding soil of a plant

Seedhead: dried, inedible fruit that contains seeds; the fruiting stage of the inflorescense

Self-seeding: reproducing by means of seeds without human assistance, so that new plants constantly replace those that die

Semi-double flower: a flower with petals in two or three rings

Single flower: a flower with a single ring of typically four or five petals

Species: the fundamental unit of biological classification; the entity from which cultivars and varieties are derived

Standard: a shrub or small tree grown with an erect main stem, accomplished either through pruning and training or by grafting the plant onto a tall, straight stock

Sucker: a shoot that comes up from the root, often some distance from the plant; it can be separated to form a new plant once it develops its own roots

Tender: incapable of surviving the climatic conditions of a given region and requiring protection from frost or cold

Tuber: the thick section of a rhizome bearing nodes and buds

Variegation: foliage that has more than one colour, often patched or striped or bearing leaf margins of a different colour

Variety: a naturally occurring variant of a species

Index of Common Names & Genera